THE ENGIPRENEUR

Unleashing The Entrepreneur Within
Every Engineer

DR. SURENDRA TAKAWALE

STARDOM BOOKS

www.StardomBooks.com

STARDOM BOOKS
112 Bordeaux Ct.
Coppell, TX 75019, USA

FIRST EDITION AUGUST 2025

STARDOM BOOKS, LLC.
112 Bordeaux Ct. Coppell, TX 75019, USA

www.stardombooks.com

Stardom Books, United States
Stardom Alliance, India

THE ENGIPRENEUR
Unleashing The Entrepreneur Within Every Engineer

DR. SURENDRA TAKAWALE

Pages. 186
cm. 13.5 X 21.5
Category: BUS025000 : Business & Economics : Entrepreneurship
BUS107000 : Business & Economics : Personal Success
SEL027000 : Self-Help : Personal Growth Success

ISBN: 978-1-957456-77-5

Dedication

This book is a tribute to the journey, not just mine, but of every individual who has ever dared to build something meaningful out of vision, resilience, and passion.

To my parents & siblings: your unwavering faith, values, and sacrifices built the foundation on which I stand today. You taught me that integrity, humility, and hard work are not just virtues, but a way of life.

To my wife: your love is the quiet strength behind every late night, every draft, and every moment of self-doubt turned into belief. Thank you for walking beside me with grace and unwavering belief.

To my son: you are the legacy this book hopes to extend. May you always dream big, stay grounded, and follow the voice within you, even when the world gets loud.

To my mentors and guides: you didn't just teach, you illuminated. Your words, support, and presence turned challenges into stepping stones and helped shape my thinking and purpose.

To my colleagues & teams: you kept me curious, challenged, and inspired. Thank you for holding the mirror up when I needed to evolve.

To the readers: This is more than a collection of pages. It is a reflection of real experiences, real failures, and real victories. May it speak to the dreamer, doer, and thinker in you.

To the engineers who evolved into entrepreneurs, to the problem solvers who became path creators, to those who build more than machines, who build futures, this is for you.

And to the divine timing of life, that brings every word, lesson, and person into our path exactly when needed—

I bow in gratitude.

– Dr. Surendra Takawale

Acknowledgements

This book would not have been possible without the support, encouragement, and guidance of many remarkable individuals.

First and foremost, I would like to express my deepest gratitude to my family, whose unwavering belief in me kept me grounded and motivated throughout this journey. Your patience and love were the foundation of my perseverance.

To my mentors, teachers, and colleagues, thank you for sharing your wisdom and for constantly challenging me to think beyond boundaries. Your insights helped shape the direction and depth of this work.

To my friends, thank you for being the much-needed breath of fresh air during the most intense moments of writing.

A heartfelt thanks to my editor and the entire publishing team for their professional guidance, attention to detail, and commitment to bringing this book to life.

Lastly, to my readers, thank you for choosing this book. It is your curiosity, passion, and thirst for knowledge that inspired every word written here.

With sincere gratitude,
Dr. Surendra Takawale

Contents

Introduction

From Engineer To Entrepreneur – The Journey Of Transformation

E very entrepreneur has a defining moment—the moment they realize they can no longer follow the conventional path. For some, it happens in a boardroom, during a crisis, or when they outgrow their job. For others, it comes as a slow realization, a persistent voice that refuses to be ignored.

For me, things panned out the same, yet so differently. The transition from an engineer to an entrepreneur wasn't just about career growth; it was about stepping into a bigger purpose, embracing risks, and creating something truly transformative.

My journey through various startups, and most importantly, the water and wastewater management industry, has provided me with a wealth of insights not just into business but also into mindset, grit, and people. The variety of experiences I've managed to amass has given me a well of knowledge and allowed me to steadily improve my approach towards both business and people.

This book is a roadmap for entrepreneurs who want to build, lead, and create lasting impact. Though it may seem so, it is not just about business strategies but mindset, leadership, adaptability, and building something bigger than yourself.

Whether you're just starting out, looking to scale your business, or seeking to leave a legacy, the lessons shared here will provide a clear path to success.

Most of all, this book is designed to help entrepreneurs navigate the transition from whatever position you hold currently to business leader.

It provides real-life lessons, strategies, and insights from an industry expert. As you go through the chapters, you're meant to gather insights and information on how startups wind through the business climate, the advantages that lift them up, and the disadvantages that drag them down. The book is meant to focuses on practical applications rather than just theory.

What You Will Learn

When you flip through these pages, you might be curious about what you'll discover and unearth. This book is meant to give you, the readers, a supporting voice on:

- the foundations of entrepreneurial success (leadership, team-building, financial discipline).

- how to overcome challenges and pivot when necessary.

- how to leverage relationships, innovation, and long-term vision to scale a business.

Why You Might Need This Book:

- The business landscape is changing rapidly—entrepreneurs must adapt, innovate, and lead.

- Water and wastewater management can be difficult to manage and develop on your own, and thus, expert insights will help you get a better picture.

- Entrepreneurs have the power to create lasting change and impact.

Entrepreneurship is a journey of transformation, growth, and leadership. This book will provide actionable strategies to navigate every stage of that journey.

These lessons will guide you whether you're starting, scaling, or looking to create impact.

You are not alone—successful entrepreneurs face challenges, adapt, and overcome.

Get Ready to Transform Your Journey

We write down little steps and exercises in every chapter to help you prepare or start on some beginning steps to work towards your goal. For now, before you start the first chapter, you can:

- think about why you are reading this book—what do you hope to gain?

- write down one major goal you want to accomplish as an entrepreneur.

- make a commitment to take action on what you learn from this book.

Action Step: Turn the page and start your journey.

Every entrepreneur has a defining moment. Now, it's your turn. As we begin this journey, we start with the first crucial step: embracing the unknown.

In the next chapter, we'll explore how to transition from employee to entrepreneur and overcome the fears that hold many back.

1

Embracing the Unknown – the Journey From Engineer to Entrepreneur

························◆◆◆························

L ife is made up of crossroads. At each and every moment in our journey, there is a choice to be made, and these major decisions can be difficult, leading you to completely different destinations.

Imagine standing at a crossroads—one path leading to a predictable career with stability and the other an uncertain journey filled with challenges but unlimited possibilities. You've spent years building a solid foundation to establish yourself in this predictably successful job, and yet, you can sense it. A pull, a nagging voice urging you to step into the unknown. Do you take the leap or stay in your comfort zone?

My journey started as a trainee, where I witnessed the company's immense growth over 11 years, moving from the G.E.T. position to the regional chief.

After this, I desired to gain exposure to the international market, so I relocated abroad for a year and worked as the country head. I returned to India soon after, and then began my fresh start with a new business division. In two years, that business division witnessed tremendous growth as well.

After shifting between companies multiple times, I soon realized that I could brave the difficult journey of becoming an entrepreneur. There's one thing that an entrepreneur requires: the belief in their own ability to consistently prove their capability and become a key person in their industry. I was well aware of that desire within me, so I shifted industries one and a half years ago and started a new organization.

I also knew I would be moving into something big when I transitioned from a structured corporate role to entrepreneurship. The decision was not easy, but it was necessary. This chapter is meant to explore how embracing uncertainty is the first step toward extraordinary success and how knowledge, adaptability, and resilience fuel the journey.

The leap from employee to entrepreneur is an essential but uncomfortable transformation.

Entrepreneurship is not just about having a business idea but also about transforming your mindset. The transition requires courage, adaptability, and a deep understanding of the industry ecosystem. This chapter will guide you through the emotional, intellectual, and strategic shifts necessary to embark on this journey.

Why Leaving Stability Feels Risky, but Staying Stagnant Is Riskier

Bengaluru witnessed a water crisis the previous year, and merely two weeks later, it would hit cities like Pune. This was a clear sign that the country's water conditions needed to improve. However, with so much necessary correction and improvement, it can be daunting to step into the industry, knowing that business and livelihood could be unsteady. Especially, depending on how well customers and governing bodies react.

Yet, we picked it up. The overarching lack of consideration for free water continuously puts the country in this state. If we don't fix it, despite wanting to, then no one would ever take the initiative.

That's what entrepreneurship builds up to: taking hard decisions no one else wants to. Leaving a familiar path for one that hasn't been explored before can be worrying and stressful. However, we had a clear principle: "High risk, high gain; low risk, no gain."

Fears, whether personal or professional, tend to hold people back more than any external obstacle does. Whether bogged down by a fear of failure, rejection, or judgment, these small, vine-like negative thoughts creep up through cracks and somehow convince us to suppress our ambition and talent and become complacent.

In our personal lives, they prevent us from forming genuine relationships with the people around us. On the other hand, in our professional lives, they hinder us from advancing up the ladder, embracing new opportunities, and demonstrating our competence.

A bitter pill to swallow is that growth rarely happens in comfort. Fortunately, we all know that bitter medicines are often the most effective. Facing fear head-on is often the best—and sometimes the only—solution to the issue. Courage doesn't mean having no fear; it means taking action despite the fear.

Before taking any risk, analyze everything you can work with. Taking risks doesn't have to be a spontaneous, instant decision. Even someone as risk-averse as I needs to check multiple times, verify each step of the plan, and develop backup plans to ensure that absolutely nothing goes wrong.

Security is great at keeping your mind calm and protected; however, it is the direct opposite of progress. In order to truly realize your potential and change your life, especially for the better, you must take some risks.

It's the common story of the man who was afraid that if he stepped out of his house, he would die — only to die within the four walls of his own house. If you do not gather the courage to step out of your house, your comfort zone, it's impossible to make any of your ideals come true.

The hardest part of establishing yourself is always the first part of the journey. In most "Zero to One" surveys, people never get past the first steps. It involves a lot of determination and grit, and success often only comes after a long period of hard work and, more often than not, perseverance. Persistence acts like the water that erodes the rock. In order to truly succeed, you have to make success the process of eroding your rock.

Things to Know Before You Make the Shift:

1. **Passion:** The most important philosophy of life is that whatever you do should be done with passion.

2. **Risk Taking:** Before taking any risks, analyze and study how you can move forward from your current position.

3. **Patience:** Impatience will lead to rash decisions. Always slow down, wait a while for decisions to be concrete, and maybe even sleep on it.

4. **Persistence:** "Good things come to those who wait."

5. **Leading From the Front:** Always set an example before you tell another to behave a certain way. Humans and employees best mimic what they respect, so the ideal way to get them to behave the way you want is to do it first.

In my 30s, I was thriving in a well-paying corporate role. I had climbed the ranks steadily, earning recognition and accolades in the industry. The prestige of my title and the security of my paycheck were what many would call the pinnacle of success. Yet, deep inside, a different calling tugged at me.

Every morning on my commute, I would ponder a recurring thought: "Am I truly making a difference? Is this all there is to my journey?" Despite my achievements, I felt a growing void. The vision of contributing something transformative beyond the confines of boardrooms and quarterly targets wouldn't leave me.

However, stepping away from a stable corporate role came with its challenges. It wasn't just financial uncertainty—there was also self-doubt. "What if I fail?" I wondered. Family and friends, well-meaning as they were, echoed this fear. Leaving the security of my job seemed reckless to some, even irresponsible.

I spent sleepless nights grappling with an internal conflict: Was I running away from responsibility, or was I running toward my purpose?

After much reflection, I realized the answer was not what others thought, but in my own willingness to take the leap.

With courage, I resigned. The transition wasn't easy, nor was it immediate. There were moments of regret and flashes of panic, but a sense of liberation outweighed them. I dedicated myself to a path aligned with my passion and sought to create a meaningful impact, even with uncertainty.

Looking back, I can say: the hardest part wasn't leaving the job. It was leaving behind the person I thought I was supposed to be and embracing the person I was meant to become.

The Importance of Knowledge and Continuous Learning

Learning is a lifelong process, something people should pick up and continue at every stage of their lives. It's vital to continuously learn different things and expand your knowledge as you grow older. We weren't ones to fall behind in taking in as much new knowledge as we could. I developed my management skill set through an MBA and later completed postgraduate studies. Having received my education from IIM Ahmedabad, I connected with many people, even more so after becoming an alumnus. I even decided to study a one-year senior executive program at Oxford. Knowledge will always find a way to serve you. The world constantly evolves, and the business world doesn't remain stagnant for long. Hence, making learning a continuous process is beneficial.

As an entrepreneur and leader, you may have to continuously update yourself and learn new things so that your practice or work doesn't become outdated before you realize it. It's common for people to secure a job and then fall into complacency, thinking they no longer need to learn. We don't have much time as humans, so you need to consciously dedicate time to enriching your mind.

However, formal education is not the only place you need to learn from. You can learn a lot from the people around you while doing the elementary act of listening to them. Build relationships with others to learn new things and broaden your worldview. People have interesting stories and experiences that can be valuable to learn about and apply to your own life.

Education is a powerful foundation, and its benefits don't stop at gaining knowledge; it's also crucial in building the confidence to make bold decisions. It hones necessary skills like critical thinking, self-awareness, and resilience, all essential for understanding the world, making informed decisions, and challenging your own limitations.

Moreover, true education goes beyond the books that schools and colleges get you to read. It's more about trusting yourself, asking questions, and embracing any mistakes as a natural part of the journey.

This kind of learning builds confidence, which is necessary to take risks and "leaps" in life, whether it's starting a new venture, changing careers, or simply following your dreams. Education empowers people, not just by enabling them to know more but also by empowering them to act on that knowledge.

Research indicates that education significantly influences entrepreneurial success. A study by **Michelacci and Schivardi** found that higher education levels correlate with increased entrepreneurial earnings, suggesting that education enhances productivity rather than merely serving as a credential.

Similarly, research by **Mirjam van Praag** emphasizes that education plays a crucial role in successful entrepreneurship, highlighting that teams with balanced educational backgrounds perform better than those with one-sided makeup. Additionally, data from **Junior Enterprise Europe** reveals that 21% of Junior Entrepreneurs start their own business within three years after graduation, compared to the EU average of 4–8%, underscoring the impact of practical educational experiences on entrepreneurial outcomes.

Understanding the Business Ecosystem Before Making the Jump

Technical knowledge always gives you the sharpest and clearest idea of the product and industry. However, indulging too much in the technical side of planning makes you less likely to take risks. Entrepreneurship doesn't have to be too technical; it also needs to focus on strategies, plans, and growth.

Think too much about the "what-ifs" of every decision you make, and your approach will become a little negative, and you may second-guess any growth you could take.

When you do your market research, be in the right place. Prices of water would vary according to where you're buying it from, like 10 rupees in a shop, 50 rupees in a restaurant, and 600 rupees in a fancy hotel. If you're trying to study a market, you need to be well aware of *where* you're looking before you think about the "what." You should also apply this categorization to yourself and determine which sector or category you want your product to fall into. You can move into a niche market, a competitive market, or a mixed-product market.

So many infrastructure and legal aspects of setting up your own business crop up, giving you a long period of learning more preliminary steps that leaders don't talk about. Tasks such as developing projects and contracts, acquiring firms, conducting legal checks, and so on.

They're time-consuming, hectic, and test your patience, possibly over an entire year, as it did for me. However, it provides valuable insight into the importance of various processes, which is why it's essential to pay attention to them.

Understanding the industry landscape is crucial for entrepreneurial success. Let's explore two contrasting case studies: one where a lack of industry understanding led to failure, and another where strategic preparation paved the way for success.

Case 1: Osborne Computer Corporation's Misstep

In the early 1980s, Osborne Computer Corporation, founded by Adam Osborne, achieved remarkable success with the Osborne 1, the first mass-produced portable computer. However, the company's subsequent actions highlighted a critical misstep in understanding market dynamics. Eager to maintain its competitive edge, Osborne announced the upcoming release of improved models before they were ready for market. This premature announcement led to a significant decline in orders for the existing Osborne 1, as customers chose to wait for the new versions. The resulting plunge in sales severely impacted the company's cash flow, contributing to its bankruptcy in 1983. This phenomenon, where early disclosure of future products cannibalizes current sales, is now referred to as the "Osborne effect."

Case 2: Emmanuel Eribo's Strategic Launch of Løci

Emmanuel Eribo's journey into the fashion industry exemplifies the importance of strategic preparation. Transitioning from a finance career, Eribo co-founded Butterfly Twists, a successful ballerina shoe brand. Building on this experience, he identified a market opportunity for sustainable luxury sneakers. In 2021, Eribo and his partners launched Løci, a vegan sneaker brand crafted from sustainable materials. They strategically positioned Løci in the luxury segment, appealing to eco-conscious consumers seeking stylish alternatives. This meticulous preparation and clear market positioning attracted significant attention, resulting in celebrity endorsements and investments from notable figures such as Leonardo DiCaprio and Nicki Minaj. Løci's success underscores how thorough industry understanding and strategic planning can lead to rapid brand recognition and growth. These contrasting cases highlight that while a lack of industry insight can lead to significant setbacks, strategic preparation and market understanding are pivotal for entrepreneurial success.

The Power of Adaptability and Resilience

In these phases, being flexible, passionate, and persistent matters the most. Structuring your business may take an estimated three to five years, and it's a journey filled with ups and downs.

Establishing your startup or being an entrepreneur is different from being a traditional business owner, with one main feature: the ability to act quickly. With big enterprises, split-second decisions cannot be taken, and requests cannot be accommodated immediately. On the other hand, entrepreneurship enables people to adapt and implement changes as quickly as possible. It's all about understanding what customers want and being able to adapt on the fly to provide it as soon as possible. Ensure that you always reciprocate flexibility, creating a relationship where both sides are as accommodating to each other as possible, making the process smoother and more amicable.

Flexibility is not a weakness; it's a strength that keeps you moving forward when life takes an unexpected turn. one of the key lessons is to let go of rigid expectations. Plans are essential, but clinging too tightly to "how things should go" will just lead to frustration and burnout. Instead, it would be much better for you to embrace adaptability. Try to work on or develop the ability to pause, reassess, and adjust your approach without losing sight of your purpose.

Challenges often come with hidden lessons or new opportunities, which only become visible when you're open to change. Emotional flexibility carries a similar weight since, as a leader, you will need to know how to manage stress, accept uncertainty, and give yourself grace when things don't go perfectly. If you're unable to do this, it could result in overextending yourself, leading to burnout extremely quickly.

"Change is the only thing in this world that's constant." As you strive to strengthen and stabilize your business, you will either make intentional changes or be compelled to change as a result of experience. You cannot stay the same forever. If you try to stay the same, the people around you will change. Don't try to move against the currents of change; instead, swim with them and eventually ride those waves through innovation.

To truly satisfy your customers, you must recognize that maintaining the same service level indefinitely is impossible.

Let's walk through this with a simple example. Let's say that customers have wanted product A for a while. For ten years, you've been selling product A, your most popular product, and customers have religiously sought it out. Still, as you reach the 11th year, you realize sales are reducing, fewer customers are coming in, and less interest is generated. As you do market research, you soon find that interests are leaning elsewhere and haven't looked into it.

This happens more often than you might realize, which is why it's essential to stay on top of what customers are thinking and moving toward.

Sometimes, this might result in you wanting to explore an adjacent market. When that happens, the best course of action is to take a structured risk. This means that when you want to start a new journey, you create a five-year strategic plan with plans A, B, C, etc.

We created a convenient " TOT " model: transfer, operate, transfer (which we'll cover in future chapters).

Ultimately, resilience isn't about pushing through unchanged but evolving through experience. Flexibility keeps you grounded in purpose but open to a better path you might not have planned.

In the early days of my career, I was working on a high-profile project that I believed would be a game-changer. I had spent months refining my strategy, aligning resources, and meticulously planning every detail. The initiative was designed to introduce an innovative solution to the market, and confidence in its success was high.

But then, reality struck. Just weeks before the launch, a competitor introduced a strikingly similar product—faster, cheaper, and with more aggressive marketing.

The momentum I had built seemed to crumble overnight. Clients who had shown keen interest were suddenly hesitant, and investors started questioning the viability of my approach.

It was a moment of reckoning. I had two choices: push forward stubbornly, hoping his original plan would somehow work, or pivot and adapt. After intense reflection and discussions with mentors, I chose the latter. Instead of competing head-on, I repositioned my solution to highlight unique benefits the competitor lacked, focusing on quality, long-term value, and customer experience.

The shift wasn't easy. It required reworking marketing, adjusting pricing, and revisiting the product. But in the end, the pivot paid off. The revised strategy resonated with a niche market that valued differentiation over cost alone. The experience taught me a crucial lesson: no strategy is foolproof, and adaptability is just as important as preparation.

Looking back, I often say, "That moment could have been a failure, but it became one of my greatest lessons. The ability to pivot isn't a sign of weakness—it's a mark of resilience."

Taking the First Step: A Practical Guide to Starting with Confidence

As s a leader, your authority and responsibility go hand in hand. You take responsibility as a leader, lead in front, and then watch them follow your example and work just as efficiently. I always stand behind my team and let them make decisions; if required, it is my job to fix things. It gives them confidence and lets them handle most of the work so that you can focus on strategy.

Keep your passion. Passion is what will propel you forward and ultimately help you achieve your goals, leading to results that bring you confidence, appreciation, and, finally, monetary benefits. Additionally, you must learn to become numb to the pressure.

Pressure is what often causes people to falter, and they may find themselves unable to perform at their full potential or make rookie mistakes. The easiest way to ensure that doesn't happen is to numb yourself to the pressure, achieve the numbers you need, and watch success roll in.

Many startups ultimately fail or struggle due to financial pressure. For the first few years, it's common for startups to strain your personal savings as well. Put yourself in a situation where money doesn't hold you back. Try to become as financially stable as possible to ensure your startup can stand on its own feet for a while.

Additionally, before any big transition—whether starting a new career, launching a business, or changing your life direction—you need to make sure that you're shifting your mindset simultaneously. You can't move into a new environment and life path with the same outlook and perspective; there has to be an intentional shift with your mind. You can't walk into a new building with the same insecurities and worries; it will only hinder you. First, you have to move from fear to possibility.

Instead of asking, "What if I fail?" begin asking, "What if this works?" This subtle shift opens the door to action rather than paralysis.

Another key shift is from perfection to progress. Waiting to figure everything out can become an excuse for never starting; you start procrastinating in the name of perfection. Instead, consistently tell yourself that clarity comes through motion and that learning as you go is okay. You can also utilize a shift from external validation to internal alignment. The transition should be guided by what feels meaningful and authentic to you, not just what looks good on paper or pleases others.

Lastly, the shift from scarcity to abundance, where you believe there are enough opportunities, connections, and resources out there, especially when you show up with courage and consistency, is vital to performing at your highest potential.

If you're unsure about putting all your eggs in one basket, there are also smaller steps you can take to pace yourself and prepare for that shift.

1. **Start with a Side Hustle:** Instead of jumping in all at once, start small and experiment. Use your evenings or weekends to test your idea, build skills, or offer services. This helps validate your direction and build confidence without the full pressure of a major leap.

2. **Build a Supportive Network:** Surround yourself with people who are already doing what you aspire to do. Attend events, join online communities, or chat for virtual coffee. Networking opens doors, sparks ideas, and makes the transition feel less lonely.

3. **Seek Out Mentorship:** A good mentor can give honest feedback, share lessons learned, and help avoid common pitfalls. You don't need formal mentorship; just someone you can learn from and who will listen to you.

4. **Upskill Strategically:** Identify gaps between where you are and where you want to be, then take small, focused steps to bridge them. This might be a short course, a book, or hands-on practice.

5. **Set Mini Goals:** Break down your bigger vision into tiny, measurable goals. Each completed step builds momentum and reduces the overwhelm of change.

Preparing for Your Entrepreneurial Journey

Before taking the leap into entrepreneurship, assessing where you stand is crucial—your fears, strengths, and knowledge gaps—is crucial. This reflection exercise will help you gain clarity and prepare for the challenges ahead.

Step 1) Identifying Your Fears: Take a few minutes to write down your top three fears about entrepreneurship.

- What aspects of starting a business make you most anxious?

- Are you afraid of financial instability, failure, rejection, or something else?

- Where do these fears come from? Experience, society, family expectations?

Now, for each fear, ask yourself:
- What is the worst-case scenario?

- What steps could I take to mitigate this risk?

- What would happen if I took the leap despite this fear?

Step 2) Recognizing Your Strengths: List at least three personal strengths that will help you succeed.

- Are you good at problem-solving, networking, or staying persistent in tough situations?

- Do you have industry experience or strong leadership skills?

- How have these strengths helped you in past challenges?

Now, consider:

- How can I use these strengths to navigate entrepreneurship?

- What areas of my business will benefit most from these strengths?

Step 3) Identifying Knowledge Gaps: Write down three areas where you feel unprepared or lack knowledge.

- Do you need to improve financial management, marketing, or technical skills?

- Are there industry-specific trends you need to understand better?

- Where do you struggle the most in business-related tasks?

Now, ask yourself:

- Where can I gain this knowledge? (Books, mentors, courses, hands-on experience?)

- Who in my network or industry could guide me in these areas?

- What's one small step I can take this week to start improving in one of these areas?

Step 4) Taking Action: Look at your lists and choose one fear, one strength, and one knowledge gap to focus on in the next month.

- How will you address this fear?

- How will you apply this strength to your journey?

- What action will you take to close this knowledge gap?

Write down a commitment: "In the next month, I will..." and hold yourself accountable.

This exercise helps shift your mindset from uncertainty to preparation. Entrepreneurship isn't about having all the answers—it's about having the courage to start, the awareness to adapt, and the resilience to keep going.

Key Reader Takeaways:
- Fear is natural, but staying in a comfort zone can be more dangerous than taking a calculated risk.

- Knowledge, industry insights, and continuous learning are crucial for a successful transition.

- The business ecosystem must be studied thoroughly before making the leap.

- Adaptability is a superpower in entrepreneurship—staying rigid will lead to failure.

- Small, strategic steps can help ease the transition from employment to entrepreneurship.

Remember that crossroads we talked about at the beginning of this chapter? You now have the insights to make an informed choice. As you prepare to step forward, the next crucial element of your journey is defining your purpose. Having clarity on why you're taking this path will ensure you don't get lost along the way. In the next chapter, we'll explore how to craft a vision that aligns your business with sustainability, impact, and long-term success.

2

A Business Without Purpose = A Ship Without a Compass

I magine this scene: You're sitting in a boat alone, with a destination marked on your map, but floating in the middle of an ocean. You have no compass and attempt to find your way solely by studying your surroundings. However, as you continue your journey, you find that it feels like travel is endless, and you're wasting so much time, effort, and resources.

More businesses than you might expect start in similar ways. They are unable to find a purpose in their early days and try to seek profits by entering ventures and projects that seem profitable. Since they don't have a specific goal, intent, or **purpose**, their choices have no intersection and don't coordinate to push towards something bigger.

However, whether people realize it or not, most businesses that leave their mark in society and become well-known all start with that one core purpose.

It's not uncommon to flounder about finding a purpose for your business; after all, I was once in the same position. It was when I went abroad to work for a company and get some global exposure, yet I could not perform as I wanted.

I was hit by the realizations that maybe that wasn't my true passion...maybe those weren't the markets I wanted to present in. There was a distinct lack of direction, purpose, and vision in my mind.

As the company established itself, I was able to define its purpose not just to be about personal success—it was about solving critical challenges in the water and wastewater management industry. It was about creating a sustainable impact while building a profitable business.

A successful business is not just about making money — it's about solving problems, creating impact, and leaving a legacy. Entrepreneurs who define their purpose early on build businesses that withstand the test of time, attract the right teams, and gain trust from customers, investors, and stakeholders.

This chapter will guide readers through the process of defining their "why", aligning their personal values with their business vision, and ensuring that their venture contributes to both profitability and sustainability.

Why Purpose Matters More Than Profits

When I started my career, it was specifically for water treatment chemicals, and that industry deals with products. However, from my experience, product-centric businesses tend not to have market views and people to talk about them. Hence, I shifted my career from a product-centric to a project-centric business soon after. On this side, the , and a lot of value gets poured into the business, especially with infrastructure. After having been in the product business for 11 years, the project business introduced me to broader regions, value chains, and ecosystems. It became clear to me that I could maintain sustainable business growth.

Being a chemical engineer, entering a business where my engineering knowledge could shine through, along with my ability to add and nurture technical values, was a key reason I found myself fitting in so well, It was the best fit for the vision of an engineering domain that I'd nurtured for so long.

Having a purpose gives you drive. It acts as a compass for your directions, so you can make choices that lead you towards your goal. Having that drive, interest, and, most of all, vision to utilize the engineering skills I had spent so long fostering is what pushed me to the project-centric industry and allowed me to build up my ideal business. These small feelings and emotions carve out a path for your future.

Your company is no different. A company only flourishes when its goal and values are concrete. A lot of this comes from having a "purpose", even for the company.

The business tagline we had decided on ended up being "no water, no life, no blue, no green." It was created with a very specific meaning, where if there's no water, there is no life; hence, without the blue, we have no green, i.e., no natural environment to thrive in. It's meant to be symbolic, representing what the business exists to do.

The main focus of the business isn't tech or IT; it's centered around infrastructure and its relation to the public domain. In short, we have assets and consistently work towards giving people safe and clean drinking water. It's not really about making profits; it's about a fundamental and basic need for humans; hence, it's more of a "service" for people.

So why are people so bent on prioritizing purpose over profit?

Our company functions well, recycling milliliters of sewage water per day and processing it into usable process water. That is especially helpful in the summer when water availability drastically reduces. Fresh water is a saving grace for so many people during those unforgiving months. We plan to serve so many more moving forward, since this is just the beginning of my entrepreneurial journey. This is our *purpose*.

Moreover, that is how a stable purpose is created. One cannot work for a humanitarian cause like this with a profit mindset. By "cannot," it's not about ability but more about the fact that prioritizing profit and having a humanitarian cause are inherently opposing in nature.

Any attempt to maximize profits and reduce expenditure leads to cutting corners, which compromises the quality of the service being given, which has dangerous consequences. This could include failing to apply necessary treatments, neglecting plant maintenance and mismanagement of profits, all of which are unethical practices. Ethics are incredibly important in this sector, and those compromises violate them.

Our primary goal is to attract recurring clients. Whenever we enter a contract, we strive to establish it as a recurring one. If we fail to deliver according to our commitments, it results in our inability to retain our clients, especially in the long term. This is what drives us to work harder and deliver to the best of our abilities. Most of the time, we're proud to report around 90% client retention. It's a direct reflection of the team's dedication, efforts, and commitment to the customers we get. Moreover, people are our most fundamental and valuable resource. My team has been with me for nearly three to four organizations, and they are, without a doubt, my most valuable asset. As a result, they deserve nothing less than the best treatment, regardless of whether they are clients or employees. After you've earned their trust, people will follow you whenever you go as long as it serves a greater purpose.

I often watched women in rural areas travel such long distances, like 14 kilometers, to get one jar of water. It's so painful to know and witness, but that's what drives us in our work as we strive to improve their quality of life. It feels shameful to know that, in such a vast country with so many people, we still struggle to provide something as simple as a bucket of water.

More problems arise in summer since it's difficult to get clean water in my society, too. We tried to implement recycling in my society, and now it's almost tanker-free. More than 1,000 people no longer had to worry about summer. That's how we try to add value to people's lives.

How a strong purpose attracts the right customers, employees, and investors

Belu, a UK-based drinks and water filtration company, exemplifies a business that transitioned from focusing solely on profits to creating a broader social and environmental impact. Founded in 2002 by Reed Paget, Belu initially aimed to provide an environmentally friendlier alternative in the bottled water market. Over time, the company embraced a mission to change how people perceive and consume water. It committed 100% of its net profits to WaterAid, a charity dedicated to providing clean water and sanitation worldwide.

Key Milestones in Belu's Transformation:

Introducing the UK's first compostable plastic bottle in 2006, displaying its drive to assist in environmental protection.

- Sourcing mineral water from mid-Wales and using UK-made glass bottles which contain a minimum of 35% recycled content.

- Creating filtration systems for businesses in the hospitality sector and encouraging the use of reusable bottles.

- Expanding the product line to cover tonics and mixers whose bottles are made from 70% recycled material.

- Contributing £5.8 million of its profits to WaterAid, underscoring its dedication to social responsibility.

Belu successfully evolved and rebranded from a profit-centric company to an enterprise deeply invested in its social responsibility. This demonstrates how businesses in the water industry can easily pivot to address environmental and societal challenges and successfully align profitability with purpose.

By focusing on this aspect of social responsibility, Belu succeeded in boosting its public image and reeling in customers. And its public image leads to coming in contact with the right teams and personalities.

Aligning Personal Values with Business Goals

There are core personal values that the company and I, as the owner, commit to. We call it the *panchasutras*, meaning "five precepts," which include:

1. Environmental, Social & Governance (ESG)

2. Leadership

3. Focused

4. Trust

5. Integrity

They serve as the key values that impact every part of the process, customers, both internal and external, and suppliers. Even employees are told to pay close attention to them and embody them as much as possible. When utilized properly, it can start to feel like a daily practice for the value chain. Additionally, since actions speak louder than words, these values help ensure that employees bring the best experience for the customers.

Your values act as the seeds you need to plant to get your flowers, i.e., meeting your business goals. You can't make decisions that don't align with your values. Suppose any growth opportunity presents itself, and you recognize that it clashes with any value of the company. In that case, that decision will derail you and take the company's growth in an unwanted direction.

Actions speak louder than words. The best way to employ those values and ensure they have the intended effect is to follow them daily, even with your employees around, and act as an example for them to follow.

Water is a vital asset of the planet that humans can't live without, so it was natural for us to want to decrease water wastage as much as possible to not only sustain this generation but also preserve it for future generations. That's how our business mind and approach to real-world problems merge, ensuring that actual change is happening and to giving people access to the clean water they deserve.

For years, I thrived in the corporate world. My work was impactful, but it wasn't fully aligned with my personal values—my desire to create something meaningful, to solve real problems, and to leave a lasting legacy beyond balance sheets and quarterly targets.

The turning point came during a business trip when I visited a rural community struggling with access to clean water. As someone deeply involved in the water industry, I had always understood the technical side of the problem. But standing there, seeing firsthand the human cost—children missing school due to waterborne illnesses, families walking miles for a basic necessity—hit me hard.

That experience planted a seed. I realized that while my corporate work made a difference, I wanted to drive impact on my own terms, with a vision that put people and sustainability at the center. The decision to leave my executive role wasn't easy. It meant walking away from comfort, questioning my own security, and facing the doubts of those around me.

But my values—integrity, sustainability, and purpose—were stronger than my fears.

With those guiding principles, I built my business as one that didn't just chase profits but prioritized responsible water and wastewater management and innovative solutions for communities that needed them the most. My transition wasn't just about a career change but about aligning my work with my deeper mission.

Looking back, I often say, "Success isn't just about what you achieve—it's about what you stand for. When your work aligns with your values, the journey becomes as fulfilling as the destination."

Crafting a Mission Statement That Guides Every Decision

The general outline of the plans we have or create is simple. There are two plans: the annual and the strategic plan. In the strategic plan, three to five items are drafted regarding what would be implemented, how the business would continue to grow, and what technology would be added to enhance usage, among other key considerations.

It's a well-discussed saying that you can save three hours in action if you plan for five minutes. This is why having a short-term and long-term plan has been so beneficial. Short-term plans typically span around a year, while long-term plans last 5 or 6 years. It's a continuous process where the strategies are adequately employed, mechanisms are reviewed periodically, and corrections are made when appropriate.

These periodic checks help keep us on track and make sure we stay aligned with the goals. Your mission statement needs to encapsulate what will always remain important to your company for the entirety of its lifespan. Our mission statement, "let's conquer the blue world with a sustainable solution," perfectly encapsulates what our company is supposed to work towards. Your mission statement should always embody your passion, whether to create something or to make a change.

Mission Statement Template for Your Company

A strong mission statement is what helps define your purpose, differentiate your business, and guide decision-making. Use this template as a guide to craft a mission statement that reflects your commitment to your business and industry.

Step 1) Define Your Purpose

Why does your business exist (beyond making money)?

- What problem are you solving in your industry?

- Who do you serve (municipalities, industries, communities, governments)?

- What long-term impact do you want to create?

For example, if you were to ask our company, we would answer along the lines of "We exist to provide sustainable water and wastewater solutions that ensure clean, safe, and efficient water management for communities and industries."

Step 2) Identify Your Core Values

What principles guide your company's decisions and define its culture?

- List 3-5 key values (e.g., sustainability, efficiency, innovation, environmental responsibility, public health).

- How do these values shape your approach to water and wastewater solutions?

For example, we'd say "Our work is driven by sustainability, innovation, and public health to create lasting water solutions."

Step 3) Define Your Unique Approach

How do you solve water and wastewater challenges differently?

- What technologies, processes, or philosophies set you apart?

- Do you focus on advanced treatment, conservation, affordability, community engagement, or something else

For example, "We integrate cutting-edge water purification technologies with data-driven efficiency to optimize wastewater treatment and reduce environmental impact."

Step 4) Craft Your Final Mission Statement

Now, bring everything together into a compelling mission statement, something that people can read and feel invested in. Aim for one to three sentences that capture your purpose, values, and approach.

Another example from us:, "At our company, we are committed to delivering sustainable water and wastewater solutions that safeguard public health and protect the environment. Guided by innovation and responsibility, we work to optimize water resources for industries and communities worldwide."

Final Check: Does Your Mission Statement...

- Clearly define your purpose.

- Reflect your core values?

- Highlight what makes you unique?

- Inspire action and commitment?

Sustainability and Long-Term Impact: Why It Matters in Today's World

Our business functions on a socioeconomic model, and sustainability is vital for its image. However, every business also requires profit since it can't stay afloat without it. These kinds of companies cannot afford to function like NGOs; hence, they need to be increasingly creative, innovative, and different.

Those are traits that always make it easier for the company to survive. That endeavor would aim to boost the company's value creation thoroughly so that outsiders can't find or come up with negatives to tie to the company.

Companies that compromise these values and don't follow ESG cannot last long in the market because clients and customers are hesitant to partner with a company representing those morals. Compromising your values and morals as a company to chase profit, at the end of that journey, will also have you losing profit as customers distance themselves.

Moreover, for our company, dealing with water, which is such a vital and irreplaceable resource, means that the care and trust associated with it need to be at the highest level. Water is an industry and resource that can never be compromised.

Quality and quantity usually need to be maintained as much as possible since this maintains the company's social impact and credibility. By recycling, a decent amount of water can also be directed to agriculture, balancing the needs of the urban and rural populations.

As we study the logistics of our job, we find that water availability is falling while population and urbanization are increasing wildly. It's causing a lot of stress on the infrastructure since before this, the distribution was 30-70 between the urban and rural; however, now it's reached 50-50, and soon it may reach 70-30. This pushes us to retain recycling as a major focus, extend water use until it can no longer be turned into something else, and conserve, recycle, and use.

All of these changes have increased the demands and desperation for some sort of solution to the ongoing water crisis. There isn't a single reason for it, but rather a combination of various factors.

However, the main reason remains this:

The Global Water Crisis. People, governments, and organizations have been talking about the water crisis for years now, with numbers getting more concerning as climate change affects the world. According to the UN, over 2 billion people lack access to safe drinking water, and demand is expected to increase by 30% by 2050.

It's due to these concerning statistics that organizations have looked to solutions with more vigor, along with the water infrastructure and wastewater management industry getting more attention. Additional include climate change and water scarcity, regulatory pressures, urbanization, and population growth, as well as Corporate ESG Commitments

So, how exactly are people moving to combat these facets of the crisis?

The current emerging trends include:

- **Circular Water Economy:** More industries are adopting zero liquid discharge (ZLD) and wastewater recycling technologies.

- **Smart Water Management:** IoT, AI, and data analytics optimize water use, reduce leakages, and improve efficiency.

- **Decentralized Water Treatment:** Small-scale, localized water treatment solutions are gaining momentum, decreasing reliance on large, centralized plants.

- **Green Infrastructure:** Nature-based solutions, such as wetland restoration and permeable pavements, are being incorporated into urban water management.

Challenges & Opportunities

- **Challenges:** High capital costs, slow adoption of new technologies, and aging infrastructure.

- **Opportunities:** Innovation in desalination, advanced filtration, and AI-driven monitoring solutions can revolutionize water sustainability.

The Way Forward

For businesses and governments, the focus must be on:

- Sustainable water management policies

- Smart technology adoption

- Investment in resilient infrastructure

- Public awareness and community engagement

As the demand for sustainable water solutions grows, companies that embrace innovation and proactive strategies will lead the future of water security and infrastructure sustainability.

Bridging the Gap Between Vision and Execution

As we found our vision, every year, we rehashed our business plans, where every team member got involved, and their experience went into making or refining business strategies. This open-door approach to planning ends u extremely convenient since employees freely throw their ideas out, we take those positively, and eventually, suitable ideas are absorbed into plans. As a creator, with authority and responsibility going hand in hand, show your team that you trust and value them enough to ask for their opinions on these plans, and make them feel important, motivating them to contribute more.

So, how can you turn even the smallest actions into stepping stones towards your vision?

1. **Break Down the Vision** – Start by translating your big-picture vision into clear, actionable goals. Ask: "What does this look like in 6 months? 3 months? This week?" This turns a distant dream into something you can actually work toward.

2. **Set Daily Priorities That Align** – Identify 1–3 tasks that directly support your long-term goal each day. These become your non-negotiables—even small progress compounds over time.

3. **Use a System** – Whether it's a digital planner, notebook, or task management app to track your goals and progress. Systems create accountability and help you stay focused amid distractions.

4. **Create Rituals, Not Just Routines** – Make time for your vision a habit. Even 30 minutes a day dedicated to your goal is powerful. Treat it as sacred time, not something you'll "get to later."

5. **Reflect and Realign Weekly** – Take 10–15 minutes each week to ask: "What moved me forward? What didn't? What needs adjusting?" This helps you stay agile and intentional.

Everyone has a unique mindset, vision, and passion. However, the most important factor for success in these industries is integrity. If people have integrity, they can add true value to society. It's these people who eventually help you identify the governing purpose and values for your company.

It's after this that you have to put work into combining your purpose and your strategies and find a way to imbibe that goal into your plans.

First, start with a purpose statement. It needs to be clear, not just to you but to anyone who hears or reads it. When writing your purpose statement, ensure that you define the impact you want your business to have and who it is intended to benefit. When your employees see this statement and examine the reasons behind it, it becomes easier for them to align with your goals and make decisions that move you closer to your objective in small ways.

Next, you tie the strategy you draw up to your purpose. It should act like a compass for every choice you make, whether in relation to your products, partnerships, or markets. Each decision should ideally work towards your purpose and, hence, ultimately align with your core values. A purpose-driven strategy isn't just about profits; it's about building something that matters.

The next level you tackle is the company culture. The culture you push for in the company or try to create among employees needs to foster a mindset that aligns with your values. Create space for open dialogue, recognition, and shared values. Hire not just for skill but for alignment with your purpose. Encourage your team to connect their personal values to their work—it boosts engagement and ownership.

Make decisions through the lens of whether the choice will take you closer to or further from your goal. If it causes a detour, is it worth it, or will it be unnecessary and just set you back in your timeline? This lens brings clarity in uncertainty and keeps you mission-focused. Purpose can be a powerful decision-making filter, especially when the path isn't obvious.

Finally, and most importantly, you must communicate consistently, whenever possible.

There is no such thing as overcommunicating, but not communicating enough is dangerous. Weave it into storytelling, branding, team meetings, and leadership communication.

Purpose should be felt, not just stated. The more you live it, the more others will follow it.

I'd once found myself facing a similar situation where my commitment was tested, and I had to make a decision between long-term sustainability and short-term profits. There was a golden opportunity to secure an industrial water treatment project for a major manufacturing company. The deal, to be completely honest, was a little insane, but it promised immediate financial gains and had a catch.

The client didn't want to adopt an advanced wastewater recycling method and rather wanted to use cheaper, less sustainable solutions.

That typically leaves two choices:
1. Accept the deal and gain a boost in short-term revenues

2. Walk away in order to stay true to the company's vision of sustainable water management

Even though stakeholders were pressing and quick profits were so close, it was clear that the long-term path was the right one. The project was declined because it was understood that this one action, disregarding sustainability, would harm the industry and the environment in the future.

Months later, regulatory changes and growing environmental concerns forced that same client to reconsider their approach. They returned with a renewed mindset, ready to invest in a sustainable and innovative wastewater treatment solution.

This decision not only validated our long-term vision but also reinforced trust with partners, proving that ethical leadership and sustainability are the true drivers of success.

Key Readers Takeaways:
- A business without a purpose lacks direction and struggles in the long run.

- A strong mission statement helps guide decision-making and company culture.

- Sustainability and long-term impact should be embedded in every business model.

- Your personal values should align with your business vision to ensure long-term success.

- A purpose-driven business attracts the right people, customers, and investors.

Reflection Exercise:
Write down:
- The core problem your business aims to solve.

- Three personal values that must be reflected in your business.

- A rough draft of your mission statement.

Start by embedding your mission into daily business decisions. Test it with your team, customers, or mentors, and refine it as needed.

A ship without a compass will eventually get lost. Now that you've identified your purpose and direction, it's time to focus on who will help you navigate this journey. The next chapter will explore the power of building high-performance teams, why no entrepreneur succeeds alone, and how to attract and develop the right talent to bring your vision to life.

3

Building High-Performance Teams

There are countless sayings about teams and their importance in the workplace. Phrases like "teamwork makes the dream work" are parroted to extremes, and this sentiment bleeds into every aspect of work and success.

Think about the most successful businesses in the world. Not a single one was built by an individual working in isolation. Whether it's Apple, Microsoft, or any thriving startup, behind every great entrepreneur is a team that drives the vision forward. Now, picture a lone wolf—strong, determined, but limited in its reach. Compare that to a pack, where collaboration, support, and shared strengths lead to survival and dominance. In the world of business, the pack always wins.

Your journey is not and cannot be a solo mission. In order to reach the goals and achievements you have been dreaming of, you need a high-performance team, i.e., people who share your vision and values, complement your strengths, and offer skills and expertise that you don't have. Let's look a little closer at why team building is so vital in the journey to success, how to build the right team, and how to foster an environment that encourages the right mindsets.

"The Right Team" and Its Place in Growth

A leader is nothing without a team to lead; his abilities shine brightest when he manages them aptly. When you sit for a job interview, every company asks, "Do you think you'd be a good leader?" Coaches tell you to answer yes even if you're not a great leader because, more often than not, what they're asking is: "Can you take initiative? Can you remain calm when things go wrong? Can you keep track of things efficiently?" They look for the qualities of a good leader to gauge whether you can play your part without much difficulty.

A leader's biggest strength is not just their own capabilities but their ability to assemble, empower, and lead a team. This chapter will help you understand how to build a high-performance team, the principles of effective leadership, and how training, mentorship, and culture shape long-term success.

The Backbone of Every Great Business

When you start any career from scratch, with a smaller role, you're just a small contributor to this bigger project that you know very little about. As you climb the company ladder, you begin to recognize the hierarchy and organization within the company. The entire entity is made up of groups governing other groups, from the top of the hierarchy to the bottom.

In that time, you understand there are very different functions of people, the reason for multiple heads that work under you, and why they all report to you. They all come from different domains, such as technical, non-technical, commercial, legal, and human resources. You can't be a master of all, but you do have the ability to lead those teams. Every other person has the capability and expertise in another domain, which helps the organization grow.

We can try to do everything alone, but there are people who need to support us in various domains and form a cohesive team aligned with the organization's goal.

It is very difficult for one person to be the master of all. So, there we realize it is your role to make a team and use every individual to work on their strengths and utilize their expertise.

In family businesses, the operations are often led by one person. They don't really believe in company structure or handing over any decision-making power to others, as that would dilute their control. They want to control every facet of the company, so it ends up being a "jack-of-all-trades, master of none" situation. That acts as a major disadvantage in a family-owned business.

When you start as an entrepreneur, the size is very small, allowing you to put your efforts and give your time to individual requirements, mainly due to resource limitations; it's monetary aspects that you want to save on. So, growth is a limitation. If we invest in humans, we achieve a result that enables us to widen the path. There is undoubtedly significant growth and potential when individuals work together as a team, allowing many to contribute to the organization.

However, entrepreneurs' biggest mistake, especially in fields a little more familiar to me, is always wanting total control. You are not the eldest member of a family business or the CEO of a traditional company; no, entrepreneurship is an entirely different ballpark. If you cannot trust your team with any amount of control, even if it's minimal during the company's early days, then you cannot be sure your company will succeed. Many teams are solidified through trust, and if you can't trust your team, they will not trust you.

Organizations flourish over time, and as teams evolve and positions shift, some individuals will remain for the long haul. Several factors may contribute to this, including career growth and financial benefits.

However, if these employees have remained with the company for so long, they have proven themselves worthy of authority.

When I assign any responsibility to someone, whether a salesperson or a budget person, I empower them by giving them the authority to make the decision. Suppose we're sitting with the customer, and some strategic decisions need to be made from a sales perspective or regarding pricing. In that case, I make it a point to share whatever cost we have, the levels we can go on, and the circumstances of references, competition, etc.; essentially, all the information required for the employee to close the deal as smoothly and efficiently as possible.

So, they have to take the call at that moment, and that authority has been passed upon them.

There needs to be transparency, not hide-and-seek or politics. While there is always competition in the organization's growth, there can't be any shirking of duties or anything that tries to pass off responsibilities as anything less than serious. Trust is the most important thing among the team.

Mistakes can happen at any point, and trust allows events to remain just that: mistakes. Every organization and its various departments have a process to follow, both before and after an order, especially when it comes to handling mistakes. If you work in a project company, there's no doubt that many assumptions will be made during project building. Assuming we receive the order and meet the time expectation, and perhaps a mistake was made by the person who proposed it, engaging in a blame game is pointless.

Once it is taken in, organization-wide support is employed. We get involved at all levels: sales, marketing, projects, and procurement. We ensure that we can optimize costs through innovative ways and mitigate risks. So that kind of culture we build. A blame game only makes things messier and less bearable; we are all human and, when we make a mistake, it should be more about and how we correct it. At my level, I ensure that i am involved in the process and ensure that the risk is mitigated.

Business can be easily considered a form of relationship management. Equal and amicable relationships always help from organization to organization. Therefore, every individual must work on their relationship. This brings unique ideas, orders, and connections, enabling them to help us grow the business.

One of my colleagues had a good relationship with a small competitor who wanted to close down his operation and focus on other businesses. At a very minimal cost, we were able to establish a relationship with the competitor organization. His desire to move into other sectors and willingness to cooperate with us helped us acquire that organization and gain those qualifications with us on the fast track. This helps us in our standing and status; we strategically acquired a smaller company possessing the required qualifications at a cost-effective valuation.

Studies have consistently shown that well-structured teams contribute significantly to faster business growth and improved decision-making.

Key Insights:

1. **Psychological Safety and Innovation:** Psychological safety is the belief that one will not be punished or humiliated for speaking up with ideas, questions, concerns, or mistakes. In teams, it refers to team members believing that they can take risks without being shamed by their fellow team members. Teams that make it a point to build a culture that encourages employees to safely express ideas and take ownership of mistakes seem to experience and induce higher rates of innovation. This safety also encourages open communication, ensuring effective problem-solving and process improvements.

2. **Employee Happiness v/s Productivity:** In an article by Forbes titled "Promoting Employee Happiness Benefits Everyone," they published that "One study found that happy employees are up to 20% more productive than unhappy employees." This study, called "Happiness and productivity: Understanding the happy-productive worker Global Perspectives Series: Paper 4" by Daniel Sgroi, published in 2015, found that "If happiness in a workplace carries with it a return in productivity, then managers and human resources specialists may wish to implement their own "happiness shocks" to help maintain productivity in the context of a highly competitive economic climate in the private sector, and spending cuts in the public sector." Many studies have been conducted similarly, both before and after this paper, making it clear that it's something worth paying attention to and gradually implementing in companies.

3. **Mentorship Developing Future Leaders:** Organizations that implement mentorship programs allow the development of new leaders, growth and practice in managerial skills, and operational efficiency of all employees. By focusing on the development and training of employees, a system like mentorship enables employees to assume greater responsibilities, manage larger projects, and advance to positions of greater authority. This investment in human capital allows sustained business growth and success.

These findings underscore the importance of building cohesive teams and nurturing a supportive work environment to achieve accelerated growth and superior decision-making capabilities.

Finding and Attracting the Right People

Startup entrepreneurs often seek rapid, almost instantaneous results. However, timelines must be clearly defined when involved in human capital and any ordering process. We can't put pressure on the team off the bat for the results. We need to give people time to understand the organization and its culture, processes, and ecosystem. People need to be patient and give people time to stabilize. Every individual is different. At the start of the process, we have to support people in adapting to your organization's culture and values, which is the most important. Once they are acquainted with your business philosophy, processes, and ecosystem, they feel comfortable and can add value to them.

When they are on board, it's beneficial to have an introductory program in place for them. HR typically conducts an introduction program for first-time users, where candidates are introduced to the team. Additionally, specific training is required for newly hired employees. Try to make them comfortable with the culture and the values we build. Slowly, we start assigning them their Key Result Areas (KRAs) and ask their subordinates or bosses to lend a helping hand to help them stabilize. Therefore, mentoring is always given to them for a few days or a few months until they stabilize the organization.

When conducting interviews, it is beneficial to pay attention to when the candidate talks about their passion and aspirations. Those are very important because we can also build other things into those candidates. By trying to understand the aspirations and passions that drive them in their roles, you can understand their motivations and how they work.

It's good to look for the right attitude in prospective employees. They should maintain positive attitudes and strive to adopt a positive mindset as much as possible, be a team player, be transparent and confident, understand the processes, and regularly engage in establishing strong connections with colleagues within the company. Those practical tips help us easily identify why we communicate with candidates.

Understanding the domain we have, the way they speak, their body language, how we communicate, how they understand, their understanding of the ecosystem and processes, and their past experience all give you insight into how the candidate will fit into the company. When we take an interest in all those things, we can gain a deeper understanding by delving into the process.

Diversity isn't just a box to tick off your list. You're bringing these people from different places into the fold in an attempt to bring in a fresh wave. Diversity helps bring in opinions and mindsets from different parts of the country or even the world in order to allow fresh and new lines of thought and outlooks to benefit the company. Each person with a different background, worldview, and process brings a fresh breeze to the company. This is also similar to bringing in fresh graduates and new workers to introduce the most recent work ethics and understandings to the sector.

Every region has a distinct culture, unique processes, a distinct way of working, and unique attributes. We attempt to conduct a thorough analysis of that region to determine the extent of opportunities and weaknesses present in it. So, how can we articulate those things that result from the cross-functioning of various departments?

You may also need to make these individuals feel at ease in some way. Help them adjust to the change in their work ethic and try to understand why there might be discrepancies with the way they approach work or their priorities. It's about communication and making it work. You cannot claim to be diverse but dismiss any attempts to make adjustments within the company that diverse employees are discussing. They're hired for perspective and change, so you have to allow them to do that.

In a previous organization, I met a project head who was said to be very intellectual, with 25 years of experience and a thorough knowledge of the domain. However, despite having numerous project managers working under him, he was notoriously known not to be a team player. He wasn't transparent, and he perpetuated many incidents of miscommunication, which led to issues among employees and top managers. This created some havoc within the organization. When people started leaving, I could understand what was happening. It didn't concern any monetary benefits or anything, but rather the kind of relationship that the project head had created, the kind of culture that created a problem. Choosing the right person for the job is critical to ensure that they don't affect other employees' experience and cause them

On another occasion, I hired a salesperson from a product background, and he didn't understand the ecosystem. Since the value of any product is very low, the project is very high. Both have different working styles, but after six months of mentoring, he has become a top salesperson across India over the last seven years. Now he possesses a positive attitude, passion, technical abilities, and domain knowledge, and is a team player. By working on those activities, we were able to shift his mind to some product or project.

Employee Retention Quick Fix

Learning is a continuous process, so we identify training needs for individuals at the start of the year and create a training and development plan tailored to their needs. We offer technical training, commercial training, leadership development, team management, and a technical training program tailored to our team. Training and learning are ongoing processes. So, we always have a lot of things for people to upgrade because, looking at the facts, the world is changing.

Therefore, as a team, we must adequately train and develop them to gain a competitive edge, which is essential.

There might be a lot of projects going on simultaneously. Hence, it would help if leaders could push project managers to go for training like Project Management Practices (PMP), which can help them gain an edge over projects, analysis, and problem-solving. I even drive for my team, just like salespeople, to attend sales training and pursue higher education. We support them financially to acquire that knowledge and give them time for learning. Any kind of learning or training employees go through will help the company in some way or another in the future. Hence, the investments are seldom regretted.

We had a site manager in the past who I recall almost forcing to pursue the PMP certification. Project management has always been considered very important, and finding someone with that kind of certification is rare. In six months, he was able to complete it. I had given him financial help and then mentored him throughout his examination process, and now he has become a successful project manager. As a 35-year-old, it's comparatively young to receive that kind of mentorship, and it helped him transition from site in charge to project head. Now, he handles operations across 10 sites in India, dealing with diverse cultures, geographies, languages, and customers.

It wasn't a decision I ever regretted; in fact, that's when you know that pushing for something that you have a feeling will work out ends up bringing the right results. Trust yourself to know when to intervene and recognize the decisions that will help both the recipient and the company improve simultaneously.

With mindful accommodation and continuous learning, communication is the most important skill employed throughout the company, and it sets certain necessities in place to ensure a solution can be rendered for anything the employees require.

I always opt for an open-door policy, where if at any level, any person is unable to deliver the reason or is sub-ordered, or their boss is not allowing them to do their job, I can assist them. We also have a review mechanism in place weekly, monthly, and quarterly. People come up with their problems at that time, and we can provide solutions. This enables us to observe how individuals can collaborate and resolve any conflicts that may arise. The review mechanism is the most important thing that I tweak.

This is another way of covertly leading your company.

When I hire people, I try to give them responsibility and authority. People can make mistakes, so I help them correct them if necessary. I bring it to their attention and help them understand what should not be repeated and how the risk they have taken has been previously calculated. Therefore, leading from the front is the most crucial leadership quality during a crisis.

If any person has a disagreement with another, I can sit with both parties and understand each perspective. If there is a means of intervention or something is happening, both can understand the other person's perspective on the same subject and why this difference is arising. As humans, there will always be differences of opinion, but that should not hinder the organization's growth. Once they understand and discuss, I act as a mediator to help them grasp both perspectives, and we can resolve this conflict to find a genuine win-win solution for both the individual and the organization.

Tip for when you're just starting out as a leader:

When people start leveraging their position, they feel very powerful. Some people are attempting to abuse their power. That's why mentoring for beginner leaders is very important. Someone should mentor them to make them understand that it is a team effort.

It is not the case that any individual can override another's thought processes. That will have a lasting impact on the organization. I believe controlling power is crucial at the outset of a leadership position.

Sometimes, you might have to deal with conflicts, whether it's between departments, people, or understandings. As humans, we experience a range of emotions that fluctuate depending on the situation. You must remain rational and avoid making the wrong decision. You must use your IQ to make the right decision, which may impact the organization's long-term goals. Additionally, you must also ensure clarity for our team. It's easier not to treat it as an emotional thing but rather as a balancing of EQ and IQ.

The best decision is to ensure that processes are clear to everyone, not only so everyone is on the same page, but also so it becomes easier to retrace and troubleshoot.

Suppose there is a conflict between the sales proposal and the project, which may make them feel like they are facing many problems while executing the project. They might try to blame the other and tell them to do the right job, the right cause, and the proper scope.

So, I developed a process where all the data and documentation prepared during the bidding phase are formally handed over to the project team upon contract award. The project team also reviews the submitted documents and related queries to ensure a smooth transition. Whatever non-resolutions we keep on the table, we continuously monitor those aspects and ensure timely resolution and support for the project team. It gets a little more difficult when it's a site project—something at a much bigger skill. When we take on any new site, many employees from various stakeholders are involved, including laborers, engineers, and site heads. Currently, we have established several sites in the eastern part of India, with approximately 200 people working, and 80% of these sites cater to the labor class.

We always have plan A, B, and C. If that kind of situation arises, we have nearby sites. We keep some key personnel ready, and if required, in the event of a strike, we can arrange for them to reach their destination with the assistance of the authorities.

Training and Upskilling: Investing in Your People

Many organizations have been around for five or six decades, developing a strong technical knowledge and accumulating extensive experience. However, as I said, both organizations are controlled by some individuals, and they are not formal teams. If key people leave the organization, it will collapse.

Your employees will likely come from diverse ages, generations, and backgrounds. There are many chances to see those from training years to 30-40 years old, all sitting next to one another. People should have the freedom to talk about ideas and views. If you are not going to take the ideas, you make them understand why this is not workable or why it is workable. However, this doesn't mean you should tolerate everything that an employee throws at you.

On one occasion, we found individuals who had been working for many years had allegedly engaged in financial misconduct with their vendors. When we discovered those issues, I began with the audit report and everything, and the moment we determined they were guilty, I immediately fired them. If you are part of an organization with a good relationship with top management, this type of financial fraud cannot be tolerated. The message is clear and loud: We can and will take strict measures when necessary.

Teamwork doesn't reside solely with employees, but also with the vast number of heads you may have in the company, like sales and marketing, finance, HR, execution, etc. If you have a strong person heading the position, you make your life easier by putting your efforts into strategic decision-making, generating new ideas, and introducing a new product line. In short, if you can form a team and they can take care of their role effectively, creating a team under them will always go smoothly. I always believe that creating leaders who are capable of managing their areas effectively and building a team will always help the organization.

Additionally, when we start a new venture, we establish the processes almost immediately. We make them understand what process we follow, how it is linked interdepartmentally, and give them the proper training for a few months. We always see a person's aspiration, which is the most important thing: aspiration and passion. What is the aspiration for, and how passionate is it? The identification of these two things provides a great deal of insight into the candidate. That is the most important thing I can say when hiring somebody: you have to look at these two aspirations.

Training and learning are particular continuous processes; if you want to stay ahead of the curve, you must sharpen your skills periodically. Everybody must be focused on individual training and development, and the organization's overall training and development needs. So, that will be identified, and people should be groomed in that direction.

In my career, I have worked with a few entrepreneurs who started their own organizations and managed budgets of 2,000-3,000 crore. I've worked closely with them and understand their dedication, passion, and management style. I learned a lot from them, and that's why I came to realize that passion is vital. If you want to and are passionate, then consider learning from those who have mastered relationship management, as this can help you understand how relationships can be built upon and converted into business opportunities.

I recall a defining moment when training and mentorship transformed an employee from an eager beginner into a key leader within the company.

A few years ago, a young engineer joined the company's wastewater treatment division. While he was technically skilled, he lacked confidence in decision-making and leadership. However, I saw potential in him—his curiosity, dedication, and problem-solving mindset stood out. Instead of assigning him routine tasks, I paired him with a senior mentor and enrolled him in a leadership training program focused on:

- Strategic thinking in water management

- Crisis handling in operations

- Communication & team leadership

At first, he hesitated to take ownership of projects. But through consistent guidance, real-world challenges, and constructive feedback, he grew into his role.

The turning point came when a major industrial client faced an unexpected wastewater compliance issue. The senior manager was unavailable, and Rahul had to step up. Instead of escalating the problem, he analyzed the situation, coordinated with the team, and presented a solution that solved the issue and optimized treatment efficiency.

His confidence skyrocketed, and he was promoted to Project Lead within a year. Today, he is a key decision-maker, mentoring new employees.

Key Reader Takeaways

- A business is only as strong as the team behind it.

- Hiring the right people is more important than hiring quickly.

- Strong leadership and a clear culture are essential for team success.

- Investing in training and development leads to long-term growth.

- Constructively handling team conflicts leads to stronger teams, not weaker ones.

Start Building Your High-Performance Team

Write down the three most important qualities you look for in a team member.

- Identify one leadership skill you need to improve and commit to working on it.

- Reach out to one potential team member, mentor, or advisor and start a conversation about building a stronger team.

A lone wolf can only go so far. But with the right pack, you can take on the world. Now that you understand the power of building a strong team, the next challenge is leading them effectively.

In the next chapter, we'll explore the art of strategic leadership—how to steer your team and your business through industry challenges while staying true to your vision.

4

Strategic Leadership - Steering Through Industry Challenges

⋯•⋯▪•▪▪•▪▪•▪▪▪•▪▪▪•◇▷▪▪•▪▪▪•▪▪•▪•▪•▪⋯•⋯

Y ou're the captain of this ship. Let's say these business waters are seas never recorded and never braved before. Imagine sailing through those unpredictable waters. The sky is clear one moment, and the next, a storm threatens to sink everything you've built. In business, industry challenges, market shifts, and unforeseen crises are inevitable. What, then, may be the difference between companies that survive and those that fail? Strategic leadership.

As someone who has led businesses through complex industry challenges, technological disruptions, and shifting market demands, I have learned many valuable lessons about leadership. It's not just about making decisions — thinking ahead, adapting to changes, and ensuring that the entire team is aligned toward a shared vision. This chapter examines the pivotal role of strategic leadership in driving business success and how to lead effectively in uncertain environments.

Leadership is not just about managing – it's about vision, strategy, and adaptability. It's about making decisions that shape a business's future. Strategic leaders don't just react to changes—they anticipate them, plan for them, and turn challenges into opportunities.

This chapter will guide readers through strategic thinking, tough decisions, and steering their business through industry shifts, technological advancements, and evolving customer expectations.

The Difference Between Managing and Leading

People tend to be attracted to success. Entrepreneurs often face a preliminary issue: since success is often perceived as a risk, customers are seldom willing to take a chance with an unknown company in the market. Hence, until they build a reputation, customers don't come easily. As a leader, this can make the first few foundation years difficult. However, it takes more than overseeing and managing to make one a leader.

When we start any new organization, it's essential not to put undue stress on the team, whether it's a small or a large customer. A proper mindset is to strive to serve as many customers as possible, as we can observe the trend of customer demand and service requirements in our service business. The attitude must be the same for customers spending 10,000 rupees, 10 crore rupees, or 100 crore rupees. As we grow, we must move beyond offering low to medium-value services, which add value to our customers. Otherwise, it isn't easy to achieve a high customer satisfaction index. That is a tough decision we must make: how to exit those business lines, focus on product lines that align with your specific vision and values, and operate quickly. As a possibly difficult business decision, we have to let go of those customers and focus on the large sales customers. Usually, we follow this organization; once we start growing at a fast pace, we have to eliminate the smaller customers and values.

Vision is most important in any organization; it sets the foundation for long-term goals. Without vision, you can't survive, and ideally, every person in the company should work together with that vision. Vision statements are crucial, and effective strategies are necessary.

Those can be short-term or long-term. However, they tended to be more long-term for the sake of being thorough. The most important thing is how quickly we can adapt to the situation. And for that change, we require adaptivity. That is the most critical aspect of innovation.

When starting any business, the founders usually start with a resource constraint. There are many things to manage; in fact, you might find yourself with your hands full of things to manage. But as soon as you are growing in the organization, people have to lead it, because there is a shift in the business frame. In every organization where we work, it is the most crucial shift: moving from managing mindset to leading mindset. It can be hard to keep a larger group of people focused on the same goal for years, but the most important thing to maintain during those years is belief. Give your employees reasons to maintain their belief.

In COVID-19, so many uncertainties were thrown at businesses, and the country's state was so unsteady that no one could tell when something else would collapse. There was immense fear and uncertainty as a company heavily involved in emergency services, where we can't shut down the water supply and wastewater treatment plant, and can't simply stop providing water to humans. Globally, the logistical problem is easily identifiable: the inability to obtain materials, yet the pressing need to run the plant. Then came the family pressure because everything seemed like a life threat, and traveling was too dangerous.

As the situation remained uncertain for an extended period, many industries began reducing salaries and laying off employees. However, we knew at the time that the best course of action would have been to be firm with our employees. We give them confidence. We assisted them or their families when they required medical attention through our connections. We tried our best to support them as a family. At that time, people were able to give their 100%. We overcame that situation without cutting any salaries or making any other changes for the employees.

It's these actions that have allowed them to believe "our leaders firmly stand with us at difficult times."

During the lockdown, the only restriction our company faced was on travel, but we received special government permission. Only then did we learn how to work remotely with people from various locations.

The technology has been upgraded, and the mechanisms we have implemented continue to assist us with our review process. Since we are largely an in-front company, four or five years ago, there was no technology focus, as people were focused on infrastructure.

However, following the COVID-19 pandemic, the focus on technology has shifted, and we are now actively pursuing the implementation of AI in infrastructure. So, that represents a major shift in strategy, and from the market, we can observe this at certain times.

Adaptability in leadership has always been crucial for the sustainability and growth of companies, especially in the water and wastewater industry. Here's a comparison of leaders who successfully adapted to industry changes versus those who failed to evolve:

Leaders Who Successfully Adapted:

Yvette Ishimwe – Iriba Water Group

1. **Adaptation:** At age 20, Yvette Ishimwe founded Iriba Water Group in Rwanda to tackle water scarcity in underserved communities. Recognizing the limitations of traditional water distribution methods, she implemented innovative solutions as well as water kiosks and filtration systems, including water ATMs.

2. **Outcome:** Under her leadership, the company has provided safe drinking water to over 300,000 people in Rwanda and the Democratic Republic of the Congo, created 68 jobs, and prevented the emission of 62 metric tons of CO_2 each month.

Leaders Who Failed to Adapt:

Thames Water Leadership

1. **Failure:** Thames Water accumulated debts of around £15 billion by 2022, primarily due to inadequate infrastructure investments and environmental stewardship. This financial strain led to discussions about a potential collapse and state bailout.

2. **Outcome:** The company faced leadership resignations, urgent funding talks, and the threat of nationalization. Customers were ordered to pay back £101 million for poor performance, highlighting the consequences of failing to adapt to industry demands and regulatory expectations.

3. **Proactive Innovation:** Embracing innovative technologies and business models can effectively address water scarcity and environmental challenges.

4. **Financial Prudence:** Neglecting infrastructure investments and environmental stewardship can lead to financial instability and loss of public trust.

5. **Community Engagement:** Understanding and addressing the needs of local communities are essential for sustainable operations.

These examples underscore the importance of adaptive leadership in the water and wastewater industry, where proactive strategies and responsiveness to environmental and societal needs are vital for long-term success.

Anticipating Challenges Before They Happen

Most of the time, we don't sell what we have; we sell what the customer needs, so we identify the needs and look at our experience. For so many years, we have been talking about how we brought a new model called **transfer-offer-transfer (T-O-T):**

As a manufacturer, your focus is not on producing water; you have to produce your own product. So the clients give us their problems or issues, in the hopes that we can solve them. We will run the plant and have them buy water from us. Today, the cost is X, and you have to go X minus 1, but all responsibility lies with us. We typically want a long-term contract. This successfully secures our business line. We worked on bringing this new concept to the market, and so far, there have been positive responses.

Being involved in the administrative water supply means we must be concerned with water quality, treatment, and power costs. There is a lot of data to analyze daily, including how efficiently we can run the plant, reduce consumption, and reduce the losses in the water. So, we are always analyzing data, and we work on the probabilities and how we can reduce the cost, maintenance cost, optimize the cost, and increase the life of the infrastructure. So, if you are able to maintain the equipment life, it is like you exercise and control food; you become more effective and have a healthy life. So, we focus on those areas by analyzing the data, probabilities, solutions, and the addition of new technologies, and we can increase the health of our plants.

In a way, I am very fortunate, having worked with two to three people who are entrepreneurs, from employee to entrepreneur. From them, I saw how they have grown in their life, what values they carry, how passionate they are about their work, how they front-end things, how they want to create a value chain, and how they do ethical business.

Those are the things I learned from two or three leaders with whom I work very closely as an employee and entrepreneur, and how they've grown.

A personal challenge you might face as an organization grows is time constraints. Being pulled between various responsibilities isn't easy, but you can't ignore everything apart from work. Time management is extremely important. A lot of your focus gets diverted when you take on a new project, especially since you need to be involved at all levels when it's first starting out. It's easy for entrepreneurs to fail in this, and it is an age-old tale to see them actually fail. Only with continuous practice, like I have with three organizations, does one learns how to manage their time according to needs.

You may even encounter issues with control and decision-making power. In my last organization, I started from scratch and took it to the level where it became a Top 20 water company globally. However, even though I still hold onto that business, a major stakeholder is involved in another business. They try to start intervening when they see that the business is growing. At that time, I remember thinking, "Next, whatever enterprise I start, I must have a majority stake and control." That was a very emotional and difficult decision to make. I had to liquidate my equity in that company and start again from scratch.

If you want to have a big dream, you require financial support, and that financial support only comes from somebody who can have that financial muscle. So, I wouldn't say it was a hard decision, but at that time, I wanted to seize fast growth, and that's why I accepted the helping hand as a financial boost. But as an entrepreneur, that falls to individual capacity. Not everyone seeks monetary gain; instead, they look for power and creation. So, I am that kind of person; I always look for that power and creation in what I do. So, it varies from individual to individual. It is an individual decision how we look.

When we create, I have that idea of a TOT model, creating the platform, zero-liquid-discharge, recycling, and PPP. When you have a major stakeholder, you bring a lot of your thought processes and experience; at that time, you are a decision maker, so you can take on this. That's the freedom I could envision, and I'm able to execute those ideas, so along with it, I started a specialty chemical business group.

We strategize as a short-term business goal, and the strategy we talk about runs for five years. Proportionally, it is not a 20-30% growth; we are talking about 5 times the growth. Those are the two things we always pay attention to.

I don't compromise on that. Only you can increase tenure to achieve more short-term goals. Instead of 5 years, you should have 7 years. It doesn't shift your vision or goals. It is only a shifting of the time frame.

A few years ago, I noticed a growing demand for decentralized wastewater treatment solutions due to increasing urbanization, stricter environmental regulations, and the need for sustainable water management. Governments and industries were shifting focus from traditional centralized treatment plants to modular, decentralized systems that could treat wastewater at the source, reducing transportation costs and improving efficiency

Recognizing this trend ahead of the curve, I immediately worked towards making our company:

- Invest in R&D by developing compact and energy-efficient systems tailored for various industries, residential communities, and remote locations.

- Work on strategic partnerships by collaborating with municipalities and private developers to integrate new systems into city projects.

- Adapt our workforce by facilitating their learning to utilize the new technologies (like membrane bioreactors (MBRs) and bio-based treatment solutions).

When the new regulations finally came into effect, we were securely ready with all our solutions. By adopting this proactive approach, we secured major contracts, expanded into new markets, and established a stable reputation as a sustainable water management innovator.

Making Tough Decisions as a Leader

A key leader should always have two things: monetary benefits and career growth. We should have long-term goals and share them with key team members because they add value, and we follow a teamwork process. So, as a leader and an ethical businessman, you should keep your word because we are a recurring kind of business; whatever order we take, we are able to deliver those commitments to customers. It is a commitment from both internal and external customers. Whatever happens, walk the talk; that is the most important thing that I can say.

If we talk about external challenges, COVID was the most difficult example. We practically forced ourselves to stay functional and to cope with that period, and I don't see any economic downturn from that, because water is a necessity for humans.

Additionally, since we are into existing projects, once those plants are built, we have to run, modify, and recycle them. As long as economic factors don't shift, we're able to stay stable. Regulatory norms are also being tightened because the government is becoming increasingly stringent on the effluent or sewage water you create, and is strict on the parameters. It ends up being a business opportunity for us to create technology upgrades—we always convert possible threats into opportunities.

It is always a delightful journey when there are economic, downtime, and regulatory challenges. We try to convert those challenges into opportunities.

The government is very stringent with pollution, so they, in turn, made the norms very stringent. As a result, many pollution control systems have cropped up. For example, states have pollution control boards, as well as the Central Pollution Control (CPC). They brought many regulatory norms, and for the existing plant, we required treatment to be discharged. We developed this public-private partnership, helping the government achieve those technical norms and signing long-term contracts with it. This partnership benefited all of us.

With COVID specifically, it happened so fast. We didn't get any time to cope with the situation. There were problems, failures of supply chain management, people being afraid, and the looming life threat. So many challenges happened in a short span of time, and nobody knew whether anything was going to work. So, that was a very difficult time for us. But we quickly adopted changes, technology upgrades, monitoring, and anything else we could manage.

Constant communication with the team, especially during a crisis, was vital. Whatever support was required, it took time to understand the issues, give them the solutions, make sure that the crisis was manageable, stand with your team till the crisis was solved, mentor them, and guide them.

Eugène Belgrand's comprehensive overhaul of Paris's water and sewer systems in the mid-19th century was a pivotal business decision that significantly shaped the water and wastewater industry.

Prior to 1850, Paris faced severe challenges with its water infrastructure. The city's drinking water supply was critically limited, and wastewater was often discharged directly into the Seine River, leading to public health crises and environmental degradation.

The existing sewer systems were inadequate to meet the demands of a rapidly growing population.

In 1855, Eugène Belgrand was appointed Director of Water and Sewers in Paris. Belgrand immediately overtook the seemingly impossible task of overhauling and changing the city's water management system.

1. **Expansion of Sewer Networks:** He designed and constructed extensive underground tunnels that were clean, easily accessible, and substantially larger than previous systems. This expansion increased Paris's sewer system fourfold between 1852 and 1869.

2. **Development of Aqueducts:** Belgrand addressed the city's freshwater needs by constructing a system of aqueducts that nearly doubled the amount of water available per person per day and significantly increased the number of homes with running water.

Belgrand's work on the sewage systems changed the quality of people's lives. By managing wastewater and providing clean drinking water, the statistics of waterborne disease afflictions and deaths decreased, allowing the urban population to flourish. He raised the bar for urban infrastructure and made waves in worldwide designs and construction of sewer systems. It allowed Paris to support any future growth, by ensuring that the city could accommodate its expansion without compromising the health of the environment or the public.

Change is constant, and you should be ahead of the competition. Infrastructure does not really have technology-centric progression, but we already started working on the implementation of AI. We've also explored the option of setting up a remote monitoring site by creating a war room where we can view all sites online, including water flow, water quality, operational status, power consumption, and committal consumption. That kind of technology and innovation is already VRA. We can envision ourselves as leaders in 10 years, and today we must start taking the necessary steps. Therefore, learning is very important for individuals who have achieved something in life, as they are often ahead of their time, making them successors and pioneers.

Digital transformation has significantly enhanced the efficiency and sustainability of the water and wastewater industry. There have been a multitude of developments for the industry:

1. **Adopting Digital Technologies:** A global survey detailed that the water distribution systems serve as a primary entry point for digital technology adoption in the urban water cycle.

2. **Operational Efficiency:** Digital solutions like the Internet of Things (IoT) have vastly helped and improved wastewater treatment plants (WWTPs). This has allowed real-time monitoring and control.

3. **Industry Consensus:** Interviews with nearly 50 utility executives and over 20 experts worldwide tell us that embracing digital solutions is seen as "imperative" for water and wastewater utilities.

These demonstrate that digital adaptation is crucial for the advancement and resilience of the water and wastewater sector.

Key Reader Takeaways

- Leadership is about vision, strategy, and adaptability.

- Great leaders anticipate industry changes and prepare for them.

- Tough decisions are part of leadership—making them wisely is key.

- Technology and innovation are essential for staying relevant in any industry.

- Building resilience within a team ensures long-term business success.

Reflection Exercise:

- Identify one major industry shift that could impact your business in the next five years.

- Write down one tough decision you've been avoiding and outline a plan for making it.

- List three leadership skills you need to develop further.

Schedule a leadership review session—evaluate where you stand as a leader and set measurable goals for improving your strategic thinking and decision-making.

As the captain of your business, you now understand the power of strategic leadership. But even the best leaders need the right relationships to succeed.

In the next chapter, we'll explore how collaboration, networking, and stakeholder relationships play a crucial role in business transformation.

5

Overcoming Challenges – Lessons from the Water Industry

I magine launching a new project with excitement, only to face an unexpected roadblock—regulations change overnight, customers pull back, or financial constraints tighten their grip. Regardless of industry, every entrepreneur will face storms they didn't anticipate. But the actual test of success isn't about avoiding challenges—it's about how you handle them when they arrive.

There is definitely no shortage of challenges that entrepreneurs face in their journeys, from technological changes to regulatory shifts and financial downturns. But instead of backing down, they have embraced each challenge as an opportunity to innovate and lead differently.

No business journey is free of obstacles. Challenges force growth, adaptation, and innovation—if approached with the right mindset. In this chapter, we'll explore how successful entrepreneurs navigate setbacks, learn from failures, and emerge stronger than before. This will help readers recognize, analyze, and respond to challenges effectively while turning setbacks into stepping stones for long-term success.

The Reality of Challenges in Business

Most entrepreneurs face two big challenges at some point in their journey. The first is the finance challenge, and the second is human capital. When entrepreneurs start from scratch, they struggle the most with arranging finances to keep the organization afloat and attracting the human capital that best suits their needs.

A third challenge that pops up, specifically in a country like India, is the customer base and reach. When you create a new product and try to market it, you struggle with qualifications, reach, and even customer references, even more so considering the size of the country.

From personal experience, among the three challenges, finance proved to be the worst of them all. A finance partner we signed a contract with ended up not fulfilling their commitments, causing many issues for the company. To deal with it, we negotiated with vendors, tried our best to make maximum credit available, and reduced the gap between inflow and outflow. It became difficult because employees still need to be paid despite struggling finances. Somehow, we can sustain ourselves in that environment, but a big takeaway is that you can never lose or slip up if you're a self-sustaining body.

Once you become aware of a challenge, a big wall that stands between you and your goal, almost instantly, you may be confused, and in worst-case situations, you may find yourself struggling to make decisions.

The preliminary method of dealing with the issue is to first write it down and then list the possible causes and solutions. By putting everything on a sheet and being able to look it over at a glance, you can simplify everything into the most important and pressing details.

Use elimination to cut out what wouldn't be plausible for you to attempt or be a cause, and slowly narrow your opinions.

Finally, you can make the most appropriate decision. This is an exercise that can easily be followed for 24-48 hours after the challenge is realized.

Apart from problem-solving at the time, the most important thing you can do is to reassure your employees. Startups are already finicky, and it can be hard for an employee to trust that their hard work will come back to them in a good enough way. In moments of crisis, they will find their trust and determination tried even further; few may even succumb to the fear and bow out. It's another responsibility of yours at that moment to reassure them that you will handle it, to stress their worth, and to emphasize how you need them to hold on for a while longer.

Financing such utility management, which operates on a recurring revenue model, is anchored by long-term contracts ranging from two to ten years. These contracts ensure stable income streams, with payments typically received quarterly, half-yearly, or bimonthly. We closely manage inflow and outflow with vendors and ensure they aren't excessive. Every service or vendor we come in contact with is treated just as well as a business partner. It's out of these contracts that they, too, get sustainable business for the long term. It's also their efforts that give credit to our business models.

Hiccups of Business

Entrepreneurs are not strangers to failure or hiccups in their journey. Rather, they're known as entrepreneurs because of their ability to overcome these difficulties.

We once landed a sizable tender, a pre-contract agreement, with a major corporation. We worked for almost six months to frame the "pre-qualification." Unfortunately, the tender was cancelled, wasting all our hard work.

However, if there was one bright side to this, it was that we finally understood how influence actually sways deals and how it can backfire on us.

Generally, any risks taken are carefully calculated, and their implications and consequences are thoroughly considered. It's also extremely natural to keep contingency plans, whether one or three. If not due to the decision's lack of stability, then for the sake of peace of mind. Additionally, as Engineering Procurement and Construction (EPC) contractors, we can see the cashflows, which is why planning always helps us minimize the burden over time in order to create that financial plan, we would make sure to analyze the customers' credentials, their pattern of payment, credibility, bank credits, and any other details that may help.

One of the grassroots refineries works in the northern part of India. Here, the plant is a water-wastewater block. Our competitor built it but could not give the performance guarantee test, so he ran away with that supplier. We took over that contract, and customers were facing numerous problems at the time. We worked closely with our customers to help them secure a plant commission. We helped them utilize our technical expertise, providing solutions to overcome the situation. This gives them confidence, fosters a relationship, and enables the implementation of an improvement plan. We stand with the client, and we give, and once he gets confidence in us, he stands with us, gives permission, and gives funds for those modifications. The contract was subsequently executed for a duration of 10 years.

Research indicates that many successful businesses encounter significant early-stage challenges before achieving substantial growth. For example, a 2014 article by Fortune estimated that 90% of startups ultimately fail, with common reasons including lack of consumer interest (42%), funding issues (29%), staffing problems (23%), competition (19%), and pricing challenges (18%).

However, those who navigate these obstacles effectively often emerge stronger and more resilient, paving the way for future success. These insights underscore that while early-stage obstacles are common, overcoming them is often a precursor to long-term business success.

Facing Regulatory, Technological, and Operational Challenges

Other hiccups will also occur as an entrepreneur, especially regarding technological advancements or shifts. Whether from the client's side or your own employees, changes, especially with technology, can be frightening. However, as we move further into the modern era, technological advancements have begun to improve frequently, leaving those unable to adapt behind.

Regardless, we always try to bring innovative solutions to make the process more comfortable. Innovation is a stage of improvement. We try to ensure the client's confidence during the process and follow gradual steps to ease them into it. A lot of it depends on building up a rhythm, plan, and confidence for all the parties involved.

At times, we have to manage customer expectations even when challenges arise due to factors beyond our control. When a plant is designed and built by another party, it often involves different engineering approaches and technologies. Design limitations or flaws can significantly impact plant operations and make it difficult to meet the required outlet parameters consistently. Despite this, customers still expect performance, but our ability to influence outcomes is limited since we haven't designed the system ourselves.

So, instead, we try to help the customers understand the situation, rebuild their confidence, and explain the difficulties and hurdles in getting those outlet parameters.

After they understand the situation, we start providing possible solutions, improvement plans, and any modifications that may make the process smoother.

This is generally how a sturdy and reliable customer relationship is built, since all of these steps help the customer understand that you are on their side and are part of this process to make it easy for them.

When it comes to competition in our business domain, we must constantly innovate and strategize our operations. When we launched this new venture, which includes our water and wastewater platform along with the model of transfer-operate-transfer, we requested the customer to transfer their asset, and we managed that asset for them. They need the water essential for their processes. Thus, this business strategy is distinctive; we aim to gain an advantage over the competition, although there are certain risks involved in this model because we are making specific commitments. Nevertheless, our expertise and team are our greatest assets. As a result, we surpass the competition, which makes us unique on this platform. Being innovative in thought, possessing the ability to take risks, and having a business strategy that provides a competitive edge are the three most important aspects that set us apart.

When we talk about Transfer-Operate-Transfer (T-O-T), there is some water involved if there is any manufacturing setup. So, their major focus is on production, not on the water, but water is important to set the process in motion. Because, as an expert, we are saying you transfer that asset to us, we will operate that plant. For operation, we require manpower, chemicals, spares, and technology upgradation, which we take care of. If tomorrow's cost is X, I will give X minus 1, but I want a long-term contract. I can invest in modifications to reduce costs and increase my profitability. So it is a win-win situation for both the client and us.

Setbacks to Opportunities – The Art of Strategic Problem-Solving

Many people crumble under pressure during crises and cannot persevere. Your mind is the most important thing to stay aware of when under pressure. Your mind needs to be calm to evaluate the situation, allowing you to come up with a solution or plan. When your mind is in a frenzy, you react based on your emotions, which can lead to hasty and unsteady decisions.

Especially in a moment of crisis, it can be hard for someone to be available so they can support you and the decisions you make. Hence, being able to calm yourself down is a crucial skill that needs to be implemented first. Actions like breathing exercises, walking, and drinking some water can help refresh your mind and help clear your thoughts, restarting a more rational line of thought.

Then you can start to break the situation down. Organize your information in any convenient format, **like a fishbone diagram, and then implement elimination theory.** That helps you narrow down any causes or solutions that don't fit the situation.

It's similar to getting a blood test when you've been feeling weak, so doctors can rule out everything that couldn't be the cause. This process of fishbone and elimination has worked incredibly well to get to the roots of every crisis and successfully fix things.

Analyzing and understanding are the most important keys to solving any crisis. Analyze each situation: why it arises, what the causes are, what precautionary measures we have to take, and how to make them successful.

A persistent challenge we face is that the Indian water management sector falls short of technological advancement expectations. So, no matter who enters the industry or how established or rough, they serve as competition.

However, often the competition is brief, as only a few can maintain long-term success. Instead, they enter the industry looking for short-term wins and solutions; predictably, it doesn't help them last. The fact that it's not technologically advanced could be the aspect that tamps down the amount of competition.

There is a three-step approach to overcoming business problems:

- Analyze the root cause of the challenge

- Explore alternative solutions

- Innovate instead of retreating

We never bid for a tender that is published. Instead, we go to clients and create opportunities. When the tender eventually comes, we break down the budgeting, qualification, and competition. We always sell what the customer wants. Following this has consistently given us a hit ratio of around 70-80%. Starting directly from the concept stage instead of following a trend or something someone else has already created isn't the kind of business we want to enter, and it affects our profitability.

This is what gives us an edge over the competition.

In my experience, my attitude towards to-do lists makes a significant difference. I always try to drive myself. If people cannot be confident, I accompany them and show them how to accomplish tasks. So, we end up automatically building a team based on your working style. As leaders, we should always demonstrate success and try to make people taste success. Once they taste success, their confidence level rises. That is what I find most interesting.

The stakeholder of my previous organization represented his dedication in such an inspiring way. He was passionate and gave most of his time to the business. It was impossible not to consider his hard work, analysis skills, and knowledge.

He had developed himself into a general management-oriented leader, where we could talk about anything from technical to commercial to legal to human resources.

There are countless examples of companies in the water industry that have bounced back from precarious situations, but a company that employed remarkable problem-solving skills is the Phnom Penh Water Supply Authority (PPWSA) in Cambodia.

In 1992, they faced an extremely high-stakes situation. Only 20% of Phnom Penh had access to piped water, and that water was only available for 10 hours a day.

Nearly 72% of water had disappeared in leaks, manipulation, and illegal connections. Paired with underpaid and demotivated staff, the crisis was a huge obstacle to development and growth.

PPWSA acted swiftly and resolutely. They introduced a strong theme of accountability and dismissed corrupt employees. They tightened measures around bill payments to prevent them from being lost in the system. Additionally, they legitimized many previously illegal connections to prevent water from being lost in illicit dealings. Furthermore, they gained autonomy from the municipality to facilitate swift response times and effective management.

Over the years, these stringent and thorough decisions have proven invaluable for Phnom Penh, with their customer base reaching over 90% of the residents, securing a continuous water supply, reducing non-revenue water to 6%, and cultivating a dedicated and motivated workforce.

They even attained accolades in 2006 (Ramon Magsaysay Award: Honored for Government Service) and 2010 (Stockholm Industry Water Award: Recognized for excellence in water management).

This swift and determined response and adaptation tell us enough about how visionary leadership and strategic problem solving can turn a failing water utility into a model system.

Building Resilience: How to Keep Going When Things Seem Impossible

You don't know when a sudden challenge or issue will crop up, but you can have contingency plans in place to ensure it doesn't hit the company too badly. For example, we have a rule of thumb of 1:3; if 100 crores is taken for something, there must be a backup of 300 crores. If one customer is a no-show, then we need to find two more possible customers. We try to retain as many customers as possible. The best example of a parallel can be Apple, since it launches a new device every 8-9 months, and a previous Apple device owner always comes in to buy the new release. We try to attain these kinds of repeat customers, and customer retention becomes one of the most important factors for our business.

Of course, having a 100% retention rate is nearly impossible, and constantly keeping the customers happy is extremely difficult. You cannot satisfy someone 100% of the time. This is why we refrain from overcommitting, even if we can identify the need and give the client a moderate amount of confidence.

If you overcommit and underdeliver, it will hit the company harder than simply admitting to the client that you can't promise success for certain things. Often, when we see people overcommit and find themselves unable to deliver, it sours their reputation with the clients, employees, and stakeholders. The biggest advice that I hold closest to my heart is this: do not overcommit.

Growth depends on a lot of factors, just like an ECG. Business is always a zigzag, rather than a straight line. If we do a fantastic job in one quarter, we might not do as well in the next quarter.

That is the temporary setback we often face, but we can work through backups by analyzing the situation. Once every quarter, we get a result, and people go to their comfort zone, making them unable to put in more effort. We then try to see how we can motivate the team for those temporary setbacks. If we do not take action at that stage, it becomes a major challenge in the future. That one quarter can make or break us, and it calls for us to take significant actions at that time. We understand the situation and have started working on the backups.

If you start with a small setback and don't take action to correct it, it snowballs into something big in the long term. So, we have to analyze whether it's short, small, or anything. We have to take immediate remedial action. It's like cancer. If you don't cut an initial state, it *will* spread.

The Role of Financial and Risk Management in Overcoming Challenges

We monitor the inflow and outflow, and then we talk about profitability—it should be intact—and how innovative operations can reduce overhead costs.

Operating a plant efficiently requires continuous input of chemicals and power. We closely monitor consumption patterns and leverage remote monitoring systems to track real-time water flow and quality. This allows us to adjust chemical dosages on the go, optimizing usage based on actual water characteristics.

By doing so, we improve treatment efficiency and significantly reduce operational costs. The same principle applies to power management.

This intelligent, data-driven approach is one of our business model's most innovative and crucial aspects. In the case of Power Saving, in one of our water treatment plants, we implemented an intelligent scheduling system for high-power equipment like pumps and blowers. We reduced our energy bills by analyzing energy consumption patterns and aligning operations with off-peak electricity hours. We monitor those things and optimize the cost, which will help us reduce overhead.

Being in the business sector, funding is provided by the government. Sometimes there is an issue with the government paying on time, and often it's very difficult to manage the inflow and outflow. At that time, we tried to take more credit terms from our vendors because we couldn't compromise the operational standards; we could only compromise on the materials. These are the two major actions we take in the critical time of cash flow management.

Being very patient is key, especially because in today's generation, everyone wants success overnight. Success never comes overnight. It is a persistent effort. Your passion and vision are linked there. In our generation, we have that kind of patience with us. But a new generation, as I see it, always wants overnight success. They get overnight success, but in the long term, it is not sustainable because of their experience and a crisis.

Almost 90% of Indian start-ups die within two years because they lack patience. They want success in a whirl. There is no financial monitoring, and no long-term vision or strategies are in place. So, for younger people, my advice is to be patient. You are passionate. There should be vision. And vision is always long-term. You see yourself after 20 years, not for 3 years, 5 years. The water industry faces many challenges related to water scarcity, but that challenge can be converted into an opportunity. That's why we are talking about recycling, zero liquid discharge, and that kind of technology.

But the competition and overcommitment are so great that many people are coming. They don't understand technology. They are not financially strong. The competition kills the profitability of the industry. That is the major challenge facing the water industry today in India.

How to prepare for economic downturns and cash flow challenges:

There are countless examples of companies falling into poor financial states solely due to them not realizing it was time to pivot. An example we can walk through is "Thames Water," UK's biggest water supplier.

The company was going through a lot of issues, like a substantial amount of debt (almost £16.8 billion), as well as operational issues like sewage pollution and leakage. The company was reliant on debt financing for far too long.

The Guardian has an article that talks about the pressing state of the company. The prime minister and chancellor had been told that its poor state "presented a critical risk to the country."

In the article, it's stated that "Emergency plans drawn up by Whitehall and seen by the Guardian under the state's special administration regime. This would ensure that it can continue to provide water and sewage treatment services to its 16 million customers in London and the Thames valley.

Thames is burning through its cash reserves as it struggles to attract new investment. Last month, it was revealed by the Guardian that the company agreed to pay a £150 million dividend in late March – hours before its existing shareholders U-turned on providing £500 million of emergency funding."

The company was clearly unable to figure out when to hit the brakes and swerve from the impending financial disaster that was developing.

It becomes obvious that water management companies, due to their role in society, particularly need to be mindful of how they manage their finances and decisions. Undertaking things like:

- balanced financial practices and maintaining a balance between debt and equity financing to ensure financial stability,

- proactive infrastructure management through regular infrastructure maintenance and upgrades investments to prevent operational failures and regulatory penalties, and

- robust risk assessment by implementing thorough risk assessment and contingency planning, ensuring the mitigation of potential crises and sustaining service delivery.

This case is an ideal example to highlight the importance of risk management in the industry and how overlooking key aspects can lead to financial and operational ruin.

Key Takeaways:
- Challenges are inevitable—how you respond determines your success.

- Every setback carries a hidden opportunity for innovation and improvement.

- The best entrepreneurs analyze problems strategically rather than reacting emotionally.

- Resilience, adaptability, and a strong support network are critical for overcoming obstacles.

- Financial discipline and risk management ensure long-term business survival.

- Strengthen Your Problem-Solving Mindset

Reflection Exercise:
Identify one major business challenge you've faced and break it down.
- What was the root cause?

- How did you approach solving it?

- What did you learn from the experience?

Choose one challenge you're currently facing and apply the three-step problem-solving framework to develop a solution.

Challenges are the tests that shape great entrepreneurs. But overcoming obstacles is not just about resilience; it's also about relationships. No business can thrive without strong collaborations, partnerships, and stakeholder trust.

In the next chapter, we'll explore how successful entrepreneurs leverage relationships to transform their businesses.

6

The Power of Relationships – Collaborating for Success

·············

I magine a single drop of water: small, isolated, and limited in impact. Now, picture a mighty river force that carves landscapes, fuels ecosystems, and sustains civilizations. You've seen water-eroded rocks, and how huge a boulder that seems to be unmovable and unbreakable suddenly cracks and shatters with seemingly just time. But water was there, unrelenting and unforgiving. The difference? Collaboration. Just like water finds strength in unity, businesses thrive when they forge the right relationships.

Relationships have been the cornerstone of business transformation. Whether collaborating with industry leaders, forming strategic partnerships, or building trust with key stakeholders, success in any industry depends on who you work with and how well you cultivate those relationships.

No entrepreneur can succeed in isolation. Building and maintaining strong relationships with clients, partners, investors, employees, and stakeholders is essential for sustained growth. This chapter will guide readers on leveraging professional relationships for business success, building trust, and creating win-win collaborations. Let's explore how strong relationships lead to long-term success.

Why Relationships Matter in Business

One of the most valuable relationships that leaves a great impression on your career is the one where you gain a mentor. However, you may also find similar bonds and trust with sponsors, peers, and managers. These are four kinds of people that you'll meet in your professional career who will help shape it.

Relationships are incredibly important for the future of the company. Have you noticed that, when given an opportunity to speak freely, employees can make or break their company's reputation? In those moments, you realize that an employee's truth can immediately pivot the public's perspective of a company.

Building a relationship requires skill and patience, but the payoff is vital and boosts your work, serving as a more convincing marketing strategy than any ad placement.

There are many ways to ensure that you're maintaining a good relationship with these people. Business is built on trust, credibility, and shared value. Moreover, strong relationships lead to new opportunities, partnerships, and long-term success.

Not every relationship is the same, but there is a distinctive difference between transactional and transformational business relationships. The former retains your positions as client and provider, and once the project has ended, there is no further contact. The main concerns of that relationship are whether the client is satisfied, whether the work is done thoroughly, and whether the money has come in.

However, a transformational relationship continues in the long term, and even without business, the two sides are in contact. Active steps are taken to build on the existing relationship and become closer.

Conscious thought is given to how the relationship can have more value, how to collaborate with them regularly, and how to benefit both sides.

While both relationships are good, building transformational relationships with people who you think are admirable, honest, and whom you want to learn from is always beneficial.

It's the entrepreneur's job to ensure the relationship benefits both parties. Try understanding their needs and goals, then always offer value before expecting anything in return.

Trying to communicate openly with the client, often first by setting the expectation right, goes a long way. We also try to ensure fairness and balance by discussing the necessary commitment. It should not be overcommitment or overdemand. Then, we maintain consistency and reliability with the client. Most of all, we try to celebrate each other's success. So, it is a win-win situation for both parties.

How Networking Benefits You:

When it comes to projects in the water and wastewater industry, they often require huge investments. Collaborative partnerships facilitate the acquisition of shared funding and resources. By dividing these tasks among different groups, large-scale projects become instantly more feasible.

- **Compliance with Regulations:** Building good relationships with regulatory bodies and industry experts is bound to help with keeping in line with regulations and avoiding any violations.

- **Technology Advancements:** By engaging with certain industry associations, you can gain access to new developments as well as ideal practices.

General Benefits:

- **Advance your Career:** Around 80% of professionals believe networking is essential to success in their industries.

- **Growth:** Face-to-face meetings are noted to have a 40% close rate, establishing itself as significantly effective for securing deals.

Building Meaningful and Strategic Business Relationships

Entrepreneurs focus too much on immediate gains. If a relationship starts, they want to gain something from it. They do not try to add value. They expect instant results, even if they've met only once or twice, and often don't wait patiently for the right time, situation, or opportunity. People usually don't follow up when they have work. We should be in constant touch, even outside of work.

People always try to maintain a relationship when there is business, and let it slip away when the deal ends. However, I always keep relationships beyond business. Whether there is a business or not, there should be periodic communication and periodic meetings. You should always try to connect with the people and meet with them without business. People always keep us in mind and try to help us with any opportunity. In their mind, it will click that this person is doing this intentional act, and maybe it's a good idea to have a connection. Hence, keeping the connection without business is also essential.

Connections are equally important when related to the company as well. When I go through the value chain, I always make it a point to understand the process of external customer relationships. Especially the process of the key person in that value chain.

We keep an eye out for:

- identification of key people in that value chain

- how we can approach them

- how we can engage with them

- making the relationship

- understanding a genuine relationship with them

- convert the relationship into business.

An effort is always made to offer them value first, i.e., the value we will add to their project. This relationship occurs only when people see that we will add value to their system. That kind of engagement helps us grow the relationship, build trust, and establish a long-term partnership with the business. Those are the key steps I always take to build a relationship. Early in my career, I had the privilege of working closely with one of my mentors, a seasoned expert in the water and wastewater industry. At the time, I was ambitious but still learning the complexities of large-scale water management projects. Their guidance helped me navigate technical challenges and shaped my leadership philosophy.

A crucial moment occurred during our bid for a significant municipal water treatment project. The competition was intense, and I concentrated solely on the technical and financial details. However, my mentor intervened and encouraged me to foster solid relationships with stakeholders, understand their genuine concerns, and align our solutions with their long-term objectives.

Rather than simply presenting our proposal, we collaborated with city officials, local communities, and environmental regulators to develop a sustainable water treatment strategy.

This approach secured the contract and established a foundation of trust that facilitated future partnerships.

- **Growth:** The project widened my range of opportunities and, in turn, also helped establish our company as credible within the industry.

- **Leadership Mindset:** Success stops being about just the technology or how much money we were able to make; it slowly started becoming about the people I connected with and worked with, and the ideas we were able to discuss together.

- **Innovation & Sustainability:** Having an enlightening experience strengthened my resolve towards sustainability and water solutions that benefit countless communities.

This relationship taught me that the water and wastewater industry isn't just about managing resources but building trust and partnerships that drive lasting impact. Today, I prioritize mentoring young professionals and fostering relationships that will shape the future of water management.

The Art of Collaboration: aka How to Create Win-Win Partnerships

I always keep communication open and transparent before I deliver my promises. Whatever commitment I give to the stakeholders and my employees, I try to make it possible. Before saying anything, I try to think it over a hundred times.

But once I commit, I will not take a step back. I have to make sure that the commitment is fulfilled.

Foster mutual respect and collaboration. Listen actively, value different perspectives, and treat partnership as a long-term relationship, not transactions. Support my partners and stakeholders' success. I always share whatever success I have with them.

Act with integrity and fairness. Always try to make ethical decisions, even when they are difficult and have consequences, but I do not compromise on my ethics. I ensure the agreement is fair between both parties and that all stakeholders benefit from the decision. I am transparent in negotiation and avoid hidden agendas. I don't keep any hidden agenda beyond conversation or discussions.

I make an effort to remain engaged and accessible to others whenever work arises. Every individual can contribute and give value-added suggestions. And whenever there is a problem, I try to be available to them when they need my support, guidance, or anything. And I try to adopt and evolve together. I try to keep myself flexible; there's no stubborn ego, insisting that they should only follow my decision. Any decision and value will be reviewed; we try to collaborate and make those processes change, which can help us become more focused.

We always try to sell what customers want, not what we have. If we can accomplish that automatically, collaboration will happen. Customers see value in us, and then they can provide us with whatever support we need, especially regarding the type of business we are looking for.

However, we need to consider how we collaborate, as there should be mutual benefits; if not, nobody will be willing to collaborate in the future, and it becomes a one-time sale. Since our business relies on regular collaboration, it is significant for us and can only accelerate our success. If we can retain our existing customers, our lives will be a bit easier, and we will become more efficient when taking on new orders. Collaboration has significantly accelerated our past success and this organization.

If we can maintain those customer years together, then we can easily focus on other untapped potential customers and take them to our feet, which becomes a fast-paced business. That gives us a strong hold on this segment or domain. We can't satisfy all customers at all levels, so we strive to identify and address any dissatisfaction as soon as we become aware of it. We use feedback, send them mailers, understand their concerns, and try to minimize their unhappiness by adding value. We keep a yearly customer meeting, where we call customers, talk to them, understand their concerns, and identify the areas to improve upon. We also discussed customer rights and the Charter of Rights, where we shared our rights with them. And we periodically review the rights, the Charter of Rights, and we add value and try always to come closer to their expectation. So, there are always steps we take to repair or prevent damage. There should not be severe damage to client relationships.

We follow the ethics of not trying to overcommit anytime. If it is not deliverable, we say it is not deliverable. So, we try to avoid overcommitting. That is also the steps we take to repair or care for the customer relationship so that it should not be damaged.

A prime example of a successful strategic partnership in the water and wastewater sector is the collaboration between United Water (now Suez North America) and the private equity firm KKR with the City of Bayonne, New Jersey. In 2012, Bayonne confronted financial difficulties and deteriorating infrastructure, leading to a 40-year public-private partnership with the Bayonne Water Joint Venture (BWJV), a consortium formed by United Water and KKR.

According to this agreement, the BWJV was responsible for settling the Bayonne Municipal Utility Authority's (BMUA) $130 million debt and managing the city's water and wastewater utilities' operations, maintenance, and capital upgrades in exchange for a regulated revenue share.

United Water oversaw operations, while KKR contributed 90% of the funding. This strategic alliance lifted the city's financial strains and facilitated the effective management and modernization of its water infrastructure.

Building Trust and Transparency with Stakeholders

Transparency and honesty are the most important things if you want to create a relationship and trust between employees and partners. Whatever is on our minds, there is no hiding or passive-aggression; we should be clear with our message and honest with the people. The effort to solve this is difficult, but it should be communicated openly with the facts.

Admit mistakes if you make them, admit them openly in public, and take responsibility for success as well as failure.

Also consider competency and reliability: try to lead from the front, have your results demonstrated to the people, and share your experience with them on how they can achieve the same results. That will become a knowledge bank for them, so they can take this knowledge bank forward and work on it more. We also try to deepen our own relationship with them so that the results will be fast.

Prioritize relationships or transactions. We must show a unique interest in people's needs and goals. Be a good listener and understand what people want to say. We should lead with integrity and fairness, make integrated and ethical decisions, and respectfully treat employees, partners, and customers. People always see respect from the leader, so it should be passed on. People always remember how we treat them, so that expectation must be maintained. We should be fair to these people in our treatment. Internally foster a culture of trust. We have to encourage people, open dialogue, feedback, recognition, and appreciation, and we have to create a safe environment where people can share their ideas, so those ideas can innovate a new trend.

You can also try to build a reputation for trustworthy publicity. As leaders, we should build a reputation where people trust our words and follow our example. Whenever an external customer has concerns or unhappiness, we have to prioritize those things and make sure those concerns are taken care of and the customer satisfaction index is achieved. Build credibility through case studies and thought leadership so people can carry that legacy.

In our industry, visiting any municipal corporation with multiple plant locations typically reveals around 10 water treatment plants and 12 sewage treatment plants. Once we establish ourselves at one plant, we demonstrate our credibility, technical expertise, and additional value to our clients, allowing us to capture a significant portion of the market. Thus, we have a single-entry point that enables us to add value across all their plants, essentially turning one customer into 12. We apply this strategy at many locations across India, allowing us to target a single corporation with multiple plants. This approach helps maintain a reputation with existing customers and enhances our business value in relationships.

When it comes to underappreciated aspects, consistency always matters. Always be consistent, build real trust, create unexpected opportunities, and show authenticity. Consistency, I believe, is a more underappreciated aspect of relationship building.

All fingers of the hand are not the same. So, if we keep high expectations and it is beyond their limitations, they cannot fulfill them. I don't expect too much from people. If you expect too much and something goes wrong, trust is broken down. It often happens that what we expect and what we actually get are two different things.

So those are different, but we should always have the plans to do those things meticulously. It is always the other side of the coin. We have to analyze the situation, which will be the learning for our next deal with them.

If there is a lack of transparency from both parties, and customers have their own hidden agendas, they will end up concealing certain information. We also withhold some technologies, since there is a chance that if we overcommit them, they won't deliver. Nevertheless, there will remain a consistent lack of transparency, something you don't want to have. Repeated broken promises, from failing to follow through on commitments and deadlines, making excuses instead of taking responsibility, and constantly overpromising and underdelivering.

Ignoring emails, calls, and messages for an extended period is heavily unappreciated. We only reach out when they need something, avoiding a difficult conversation instead of addressing issues head-on.

And finally, discussing your input or not valuing your expertise, taking credit for your work ideas, and talking down to you and others in a relationship. Unethical, dishonest business practices or questionable ethics lead you to cut corners and compromise values, resulting in frequent disputes with other partners and stakeholders.

One-sided relationships always involve asking a favor but never reciprocating. You only see what he can get out of that instead of what he can also add value, making up everything about their benefit without considering yours, taking advantage of your time, resources, and expertise. Resistance to feedback or growth, getting defensive instead of addressing concerns, and blaming others instead of taking responsibility are all ways to adopt or improve the relationship. These are the few things that are alarming situations, and we should see how we can tackle those situations.

Integrity is the most important aspect, and in my career, I have never gone through a situation where we lost any business relationship due to integrity. Due to our integrity, commitment, passion, and trustworthiness, we consistently excel in this area.

With our new water and wastewater platform, we added one more business line of specialty chemicals. So we went with backward integration, and we started manufacturing specialty chemicals. When we go to the customer and talk about it, we don't have much reference, but whatever integrity we build on our specific operation business, customers always help us to get those orders, and we get a lot of orders. Our first year was when we created so many references for specialty chemicals, which is only due to our integrity.

Being in an ongoing revenue-generating model or a Predictive/Continuous revenue-generating model, our existing retention is our major focus, which has allowed us to ensure the customers always stay with us. Our growth engine truly is retention. Retention only happens with trust in the business because if customers have trust in you, they will stay with you for life. That is a major trust; our retention is 70% to 80% in this industry. That is something important to us.

Networking vs. Relationship Building

People are ignoring offline networking, utilizing platforms like LinkedIn to connect with industry leaders, and then face an inactive or incomplete online presence. So, people do not keep their LinkedIn profiles, a professional social business where a lot of insights are shared, and many industry leaders are watching. Most people are not active on that; they only network in their comfort zone. They do not come out of their comfort zone and stretch themselves beyond their abilities.

They do not affirm values, and people do not always give a clear message when there is a relationship with external customers. I can see people lacking a clear message or not giving it to the right people. Those are the most important aspects I can see.

I meet people, whether they are in business or not; there are various methods by which we can stay in touch with people outside of business. When I started this, most of the people I personally just went to talk about my new venture, what value we will add to their business, what the platform is, and how it will make a social impact. People see value in that, so that is the first six months I have done only this kind of thing, where I go and wait, meet with people without any business, make them understand what we are and how we want to talk about it. So definitely they keep all those things in mind. We greet them when there is a festive season, or that kind of connection we always make.

I can mention a few names, including Satya Nadella, CEO of Microsoft, for his leadership in AI and cloud computing, and his focus on empathy in interaction and business. We can learn from Satya Nadella.

Reid Hoffman, from LinkedIn, would be invaluable. His expertise in scaling businesses and networking would explain how LinkedIn can build a network like this. This idea has emerged and become a global platform for businesses.

Then Elon Musk, to explore AI applications in space and transportation. Only the concept he brought in, he is not that much qualified, but how the concept can be converted into reality by his passion, and how we can manage his resources. And now he is talking about transportation in space. Those are the few leaders from whom we can learn a lot of things. So, AI can be next because now, in the next decade, the next 100 years, people will only talk about ABCDE. A is AI, B is biotechnology, C is crypto, D is drone, and E is electric mobility.

So, these are the spaces where water technology is also going to get a lot of insight from this. As I said, we are getting a lot of technology updates, such as AI implementation and monitoring a plant online by sitting in the war room. Therefore, technology-driven businesses and any segment of the water industry will also undergo significant changes, and we are taking proactive steps to integrate those technologies into our business.

External customers: By demonstrating the capability, integrity, and value validation of what we have done, we can retain 70 to 80 percent of customers. Retention comes from making them feel seen and considered, something we imbibe heavily.

Internal customer: Almost all teams have followed me through the last three organizations, thanks to my entrepreneurial endeavors. That shows I have a strong relationship with internal customers as well. The retention rate demonstrates the external customer's loyalty, and people are following my vision and passion for the organization, which reflects the internal relationship. It is the most important and valuable thing I am able to drive.

Mentors are not limited to industry mentors; others can always teach you important lessons. The customer also acts like a mentor of sorts, from whom we learn a lot of things. There are Key Decision people with whom I have a strong relationship. On the customer end, they also teach, guide, and give us new learning opportunities. So, we can convert that opportunity into a business opportunity. A few customers, through our relationship, did serve as mentors who helped me in my career. They gave me the opportunity, kept their trust, and took a risk on me by offering a new position in these critical areas.

Technology plays a very important role, and it facilitates and speeds up connections. Social media, such as LinkedIn and Twitter, allow people to connect instantly regardless of location.

AI-driven tools help identify and recommend potential connections. VCs and messaging apps make maintaining relations more convenient. Technology provides more accessibility to:

- Network

- Virtual conference

- Online communication

- allow people to connect without physical travel

- Content sharing

- Blogs

- Podcasts

- Webinars

To increase transparency and trust:
1. Online reviews, testimonials, and digital footprints help vast potential partners.

2. Blockchain and smart contracts add security and accountability to business dealings.

3. Repetitive management tools help us maintain our professional and business credibility.

These are the few things that technology can bring us.

Stay in touch regularly with customers, offer help, and provide insights. Before asking for favors, show genuine interest in their work and success, clearly communicate your goals, and let them know what you are working on and what opportunities you are viewing. Whether it is an introduction, collaboration, or advice, make it easy for them to help provide context and key details. Ask for an introduction strategically. Identify mutual connections and benefits, personalize your request, follow up, and show gratitude. When you collaborate, see how it can be a minimum situation with both parties; it is not one side's gain; it should be both sides' gain, and then you collaborate well with them. And keep the relationship reciprocally valuable. So, those are the important aspects. Maintaining strong business relationships is crucial for long-term success. While the specific "5-50-100 rule" isn't widely documented, the concept of systematically engaging with key contacts at regular intervals is a recognized strategy in relationship management. Here's a practical framework to consider:

1. **Segment Your Contacts:** Tier 1, High-Priority Contacts (top clients, strategic partners, and key stakeholders), Tier 2, Mid-Priority Contacts (regular clients, suppliers, and associates, and Tier 3, Low-Priority Contacts (acquaintances and peripheral contacts).

2. **Establish Engagement Intervals:** Interact every 30 days or so to maintain a connection with the person, once every two months to keep the relationships in the back of their mind, and once every three months to vaguely be on their radar.

3. **Narrow the Scope of your Engagement:** Go for personalized communication like tailored emails addressing specific interests, scheduled meetings, maybe in the form of regular check-ins, vital meetings, lunch meetings, and share resources, like news articles, papers, or resources from their industry. This can make them feel like you are

genuinely interested in them and their work, allowing smooth conversations to flow.

4. **Use Technology at Hand:** Try to employ the customer management tools at your disposal to track interactions. Features like automated alerts help with important dates like anniversaries and birthdays.

5. **Employ the Feedback Loop:** Consistently seek out feedback to understand whether your actions are reaping any benefits or outputs. As and when you receive feedback, you can tweak your approach while also taking into consideration each client's specialties.

Implementing a structured approach to relationship maintenance ensures consistent and meaningful interactions, fostering trust and mutual growth.

Key Reader Takeaways

- Strong relationships create opportunities and drive long-term business success.

- Trust and credibility are the foundation of sustainable relationships.

- Networking is about connections, but true success comes from relationship-building.

- Strategic collaborations and partnerships can accelerate growth exponentially.

- Win-win relationships are the most sustainable and valuable in business.

Reflection Exercise:
- List the five most valuable relationships in your professional life.

- Identify one person you should reconnect with to strengthen your network.

- Define a strategy to add value to a key relationship in your industry.

This week, contact one new potential mentor, partner, or industry leader and start a meaningful conversation.

Like a river that grows stronger with its tributaries, your business will thrive when you cultivate the right relationships. However, relationships alone are not enough; you also need innovation to stay ahead in an evolving world. In the next chapter, we will explore how embracing innovation, technology, and future trends can propel your business to the next level.

7

Embracing Innovation – The Future of Water Management

·····■·■·■·■·■·■·■·■·❮❮❮❯❯·❯·■·■·■·■·■·■·■·■·····

Picture two businesses operating in the same industry. One sticks to traditional methods, avoiding change due to fear of failure. The other embraces innovation, experimenting with new technologies and adapting to changing market demands. Fast forward ten years—one is leading the industry, while the other has faded. What made the difference? The ability to innovate.

Embracing change is not a choice; it's a necessity. Leaders must stay ahead of the curve in industries like water and wastewater management, where technological advancements and sustainability concerns are shaping the future. In this chapter, we explore why innovation is the key to long-term business survival and how to build a culture of continuous improvement.

Innovation is not just about adopting new technology; it's about thinking differently, anticipating future trends, and continuously improving business processes. This chapter will guide readers through cultivating an innovation-driven mindset, integrating emerging technologies, and staying ahead in a rapidly changing world.

Why Innovation is Essential for Business Survival

Innovation keeps the company alive. It's infinitely easier for startups to switch things around, try new things, and develop creative solutions. For example, it's often required to change a few chemicals because the turbidity of water treatment plants in the East region is very high during monsoons. So, there will be small chemical dosing changes during the monsoon season. On a laboratory scale, we have a small laboratory pilot where, every shift, our chemists analyze the parameters and change the chemical dosage accordingly.

During the monsoon season, high turbidity leads to significant chemical usage, resulting in considerable "chemical savings" that translate into cost reductions. Consequently, employing laboratory-scale equipment enhances our profitability by allowing detailed shift analyses. This approach enables efficient plant operation and minimizes chemical dosage.

The operation people tend to be more concerned about their comfort zone if there are any new additions. They feel it's a headache when processes are set, and there is a change, and then there might be some backtracking or undoing. There's always a resistance to any change for any person because, after working in a specific routine for so many years, we tend to settle into the same mindset. There is always some resistance at the operational level when we try to make any innovative change.

So why is innovation so necessary for companies?

Innovation has always been the root of bettering processes and is critical for shaking things up in the company. When processes and people stagnate, they become blind to how they can improve. Keeping up with the industry and identifying opportunities to improve any method or machinery always goes a long way with startups. After all, the appeal of this kind of organization is the ability to pivot whenever and however possible.

We adopted the latest technology about seven years ago. Whenever new technology emerges, we strive to upgrade it appropriately to achieve what we call innovation. The government changes the norms regarding power factor saving and process improvement, so we adjust accordingly. Retrofit is also one of our main strengths. Thus, retrofit leads to innovation. Improvement is a continuous process, and we innovate by implementing all those updated technologies, allowing us to sustain these advancements in the long term.

At one of the North sector refineries, we took control of a plant previously operated by a competitor. This plant featured zero liquid discharge technology. However, upon our takeover, we discovered that it wasn't functioning as expected. With the support of our research and development team, we piloted these technologies and enhanced operations through equipment modifications and improved methods. After six months, we successfully achieved zero liquid discharge, eliminating waste from the plant and addressing design flaws. This not only benefited our client but also provided valuable insights for us regarding new technology and innovation.

Bringing back the Phnom Penh Water Supply Authority, they took swift action to embrace innovation and pivot the moment they realized that something needed to be done to restore access to water for the people. Not only was it quick thinking, but the authority clearly realized the devastating effects this would have on the livelihood of the residents, and maintained that as a priority large enough to warrant change. Since the decline was due to outdated infrastructure, inadequate management, and lack of state-of-the-art practices, it needed to go through significant overhauls, which did happen after 1993. This easily turned the PPWSA into a model utility.

To counter this, as previously mentioned, Thames Water went down the exact opposite route and ended up drowning themselves in debt.

Their refusal to open their eyes and truly understand the terrible state the company was in ended up dragging them down even further, leading to them being penalized for £57 million for failing to meet environmental targets, particularly in reducing sewage spills. Two other companies, Anglian Water and Yorkshire Water, faced similar penalties for their shortcomings. They were supposed to reach around 30% reduction by 2025 but only managed 2%, displayed obvious redundancy and stagnancy.

These cases underscore the critical importance of innovation in the water and wastewater industry. Organizations that fail to adopt new technologies and practices risk operational inefficiencies, regulatory penalties, and diminished public trust.

The Role of Technology in the Water and Wastewater Industry

The water and wastewater sector has undergone major transformations over the years due to increasingly stringent environmental regulations and proactive measures by regulatory bodies aimed at environmental conservation. Central authorities are implementing pollution control laws to safeguard rivers, frequently updating the standards to facilitate the rapid adoption of advanced technologies.

Some technologies, such as membrane filtration, UV disinfection, and smart monitoring systems, must be adopted quickly. Automation and data analytics have also transformed operations, making systems more efficient and predictive. So, to keep up with all this, we must adapt very fast, all while considering the environmental norms. In my career, I have seen a lot of technological advancements, and we have to upgrade our knowledge and be faster to adapt to the technology and its implementation.

In the water-wastewater industry, major innovations come from the competition. Everybody has research and development, innovation, and processes, and wants to optimize the cost spread. People always discuss technology upgrades, digital monitoring systems, or costs in the competitive market.

In the industry, there is a process of desalination, where the seawater has to be converted into drinkable water. This is because looking at the water scarcity, everybody is looking for smart and cost-effective solutions. Such companies implement the models, which are forceful against all the competition, because to stay in the market, they need remain relevant in a price-competitive technology age. When the competitor introduces any technology upgrade or an AI-driven predictive maintenance system, it drastically reduces the downtime at a cost. So many times it has happened, which makes innovation a strange industry-wide benefit for all companies.

People previously followed two maintenance models in the operation business: preventive maintenance and breakdown maintenance. Then, multinational companies came up with a new model, which was dubbed the "predictive" maintenance model. This was a new idea for monitoring maintenance in a part of our country. So, almost immediately, we knew we had to upgrade our technology and monitoring system to predictive maintenance.

Staying updated in the water and wastewater industry requires a mix of continuous learning, networking, and leveraging industry resources. Some common provisions for staying informed include attending industry conferences and trade shows. There are numerous conferences, such as American Water Works and local water intelligence, where people showcase their latest technologies globally. We take part in that.

1. **Professional Association:** Many of us are members of water and wastewater clubs. These clubs continuously upgrade with

new global technologies and share knowledge, which we have the privilege to utilize.

2. **Technical Journals and Publications**: Continuously reading industry journals such as Water-Involved Research or the General American Water Association helps us stay current with emerging trends.

3. **Online Courses and Webinars:** Many industry experts conduct online webinars to share cross-functional knowledge, and we participate in them.

4. **Networking and Peer Collaboration:** We have weekly and monthly meetings, and we share the on-site experience with each other.

We also do a lot of in-house learning. We receive regular updates from the government, where we discuss what new policies the government is developing and how it is upgrading and preserving water resources. So, those are the few methods we follow to upgrade the trends in the industries and technologies.

Personal Experience: How Technology Transformed a Water Project

I recall a project where I had to implement water monitoring systems for a large municipal water supply network.

The situation was as follows: The city had been struggling with a situation known as "high non-revenue water" (NRW). This meant the water that was lost due to leaks, theft, and meter inaccuracies. Naturally, these losses led to financial losses, water shortages, and inefficiencies.

Some of the major challenges that we faced were:
- Old infrastructure, which resulted in constant leaks and pipe bursts.

- Slow response time due to manual monitoring

- Little real-time data, which undoubtedly led to inefficient processes.

In order to combat these issues, we integrated some processes and features, including but not limited to:
- Sensors installed across the pipeline network that would help with detecting leaks.

- Alert systems that would send notifications to the maintenance team. That would help bring up their response times.

- AI-driven models that analyzed patterns. It would assist them in predicting possible or future leaks.

All the inclusions allowed us to witness many positive outcomes, like:
- The total percentage of non-revenue water dropped from 35% to 18% in just two years.

- Leak repair response time rapidly decreased from 48 hours to under 6 hours.

Creating a Culture of Innovation in Your Business

We assign a Key Result Area (KRA) to each employee, particularly those involved in projects, proposals, and processes. Within their KRA, they receive ratings focused on innovation. These ratings reflect their performance improvements over each quarter and year, highlighting how their sites have adopted new technologies and innovative methods that lower costs and enhance customer satisfaction scores. Our culture has always been a cornerstone of our monthly meetings. With numerous sites throughout India, site heads share their experiences and the strategies they used to enhance their processes. This information is then exchanged among team members.

As a result, everyone observes, gathers insights, and works to incorporate these practices into their own sites. Through this approach, we maintain our culture of innovation within the organization.

There is a lot of pressure on profitability ratios, too. Innovation always helps us reduce resources and increase efficiency, which leads to profitability. We have to make our employees understand that if people are not innovative, they are not going to survive in the market, considering the competition and the pressure of pricing. That way, we make them understand, help them, and support them in executing.

When we talk about our own organization, cultivating the culture of continuous learning and adaptability in a water-based industry is essential to keeping up with evolving regulations, technologies, and operational challenges. There are a few effective strategies we follow:

- **Encourage ongoing training and development:** Provide access to industry certification from a few water associations, like the American Water and Wastewater Association, and state operator licenses. We offer regular workshops, webinars, and cross-training programs on new technologies and best practices throughout the organization. We maintain this on a monthly basis.

- **Utilizing knowledge for collaborative growth:** Engage in team discussions to exchange cross-functional expertise. As we operate numerous plants, this facilitates invaluable knowledge share.

We also promote interdepartmental collaboration among our employees across various business aspects. Some individuals need commercial insight, while others seek technical expertise, making our cross-functional knowledge sharing essential.

- **Stay ahead of industry trends:** Subscribe to publications, attend trade shows, and network with peers. We collaborate with universities and research institutions on pilot projects focused on emerging technologies, conducting research and development alongside their technical teams.

- **Foster a growth mindset:** Encourage employees to experiment with new ideas and process improvement without fear of failure, which leads to innovation. We recognize and reward those who take the initiative and learn and apply new skills.

Let's look at an example of how innovative culture can help boost your success in the water and wastewater industry. Xylem, a company established in 2011, has grown into a global leader in water technology. It operates in over 150 countries and in 2024, its revenues reached almost $8.6 billion. So, what are the moves Xylem took to maintain their success and position?

First, in May 2023, Xylen completed the acquisition of "Evoqua," a water technology company committed to addressing various water-related challenges. This acquisition made Xylem + Evoqua the world's largest pure-play water technology company. Together, they had over 22,000 employees worldwide.

Then, Xylem invested in cutting-edge technology, like smart infrastructure and data analytics. This helped them enhance their water management not just in terms of efficiency but also in sustainability.

Finally, they also teamed up with partners in Bavaria to launch "Reuse Brew". This was an initiative to raise awareness of the opportunities that recycled water could bring to the table. Their collaborators were the Chair of Brewery and Beverage Technology at the Technical University of Munich (TUM) and the Chair of Urban Water Systems Engineering at TUM. Xylem has provided information in detail on their website. The project showcases innovative approaches to water reuse and public engagement.

So what benefits did these actions bring to Xylem?

For starters, their revenue has steadily increased over the years, keeping their market position steady.

These innovative choices have allowed them to debut on the Fortune 500 list in 2024 (at rank #486), highlighting their impact.

They have also managed to set benchmarks and standards for how a company in the industry should approach innovation and adaptation. All of their choices carry the same message: that innovative company culture is a key in achieving long-term success.

Overcoming Resistance to Change in an Organization

Innovation is very important in any domain. If you are not innovative, you are like Nokia. Nokia had a 90% mobile market share when it entered the mobile market, but Nokia is not an innovative company. Slowly, the global market watched Nokia fizzle away into a mere shadow of its former glory. In any domain, if you are not able to innovate or invest in new technology, you will follow Nokia's path. So, you have to be ahead of the curve. You must introduce a technology upgrade or an innovative method to improve processes.

We should focus on innovation, because innovation is the mother of any addition of new technology. We should not always follow a stepwise method for innovation. Innovation is a slow improvement. We have to phase out improvement plans to be worked out and implemented when we have the confidence and a step-by-step method.

Resistance to change is common in the wastewater industry, especially when new technologies or regulations require significant investment or operational adjustments. People are very reluctant because it involves the cost and operational adjustments. Due to cost complexity, many utilities and companies initially restricted automation, AI-driven monitoring, or strict discharge limits.

However, those who embraced the changes often saw improvement, efficiency, compliance, and cost savings over time. In the water industry, we always see whether there is a change in government norms or a parametric tool model because it will cost money and require some operational expertise. So, there is always hesitation.

Quantitative Metrics:

To evaluate new markets or customers, there are certain quantitative and qualitative aspects that need to be taken into consideration. For example:

- The kind of regulations in place (Are there any upcoming? Are they strict? Are new solutions required?)

- How does the market's size and projected growth look?

- Are there any companies investing in projects?

- What kind of costs and returns can you expect from entering this industry and working on these projects?

- Who is your competition, and how harsh is it? Is it difficult for newbies to take off, or is it a beginner-friendly industry?

Qualitative Indicators:
- What are things to keep in mind from the customer's perspective? Is there an infrastructural correction that can be made?

- Are customers open to adjusting to new technology all over again?

- Are any regulatory boards being forced to comply or upgrade?

- Are all agencies and companies focusing on sustainability and resilience in their strategies?

One of the most challenging moments in my leadership journey was my task of convincing stakeholders and employees to adopt smart water management technology.

Our company was managing a large-scale wastewater treatment plant, but there were many inefficiencies, notably due to manual monitoring, frequent breakdowns, and high operational costs. We proposed implementing IoT-based real-time monitoring and predictive maintenance to enhance efficiency. However, we were met with quite a lot of resistance from employees who feared job displacement, stakeholders who were skeptical about the initial investment costs and ROI, and regulators, who needed assurance that the system would meet compliance standards. Instead of pushing the idea aggressively, we took a collaborative approach, presenting a data-driven cost-benefit analysis that showed that the investment would pay off within three years through reduced maintenance and energy savings.

We assured them that rather than replacing jobs, there would be active efforts towards upskilling employees, and showing them how technology could simplify their work and improve safety. We even managed to hold a small-scale trial to demonstrate tangible efficiency gains.

Eventually, we were able to successfully implement the systems on a full scale, the stakeholders approved, the employees adapted well, and just as forecasted, the plant's efficiency increased by 30%.

Real leadership has never been about forcing change but rather about guiding people through it.

Developing an Agile Mindset to Navigate Uncertainty

When we make quick yet effective decisions in the water and wastewater industry, we require balanced data-driven analysis, experience, and risk management. When we take any strategic decision on this, we talk about:

- When discussing online monitoring, we use real-time monitoring systems like SCADA or IoT sensors to assess application performance.

- Before investing, consider regulatory trends, cost-benefit ratios, and return on investment.

- In this segment, we run what-if scenarios to evaluate the potential impact of different choices. Once we identify the worst-case scenario, we finally develop contingency plans.

- Consult engineers, regulatory experts, and industry peers for quick evaluation. Engage with a professional network like the American Water Association or GWI to stay informed about best practices.

- User-structure approach like ATV integral, where we focus on 20% of factors that drive 80% of outcomes.

We apply a decision matrix to quickly compare multiple options based on cost, compliance, and efficiency criteria.

Balancing short-term and long-term goals, we ensure that rapid decisions align with long-term sustainability and regulatory compliance. Consider both immediate cost savings and future operational resilience. So these are the balances in short-term and long-term goals we follow and the decision-making framework.

Utilize technical tools and automation. For example, in today's technology operation, we implement smart monitoring systems like SCADA and IoT systems to provide real-time learning opportunities and use AI-driven productive maintenance to improve decision-making and adaptability.

So, these are the few things we implement in our own organization

Making a difficult business pivot in water and waste for the industry requires a structural approach to minimize risk and ensure long-term success. So, we follow certain steps.

i) Identify the need for change: As industry shifts, our regulatory changes, new technologies, and our market description force pure, valid performance metrics in the current strategic leading, declining revenue inefficiencies, or compliance risks. Then, we gather stakeholder input and engage with employment, customers, and industry experts to evaluate the need for change.

ii) Defining goal and outcome: We ask ourselves a few questions. What is the new direction? Are we shifting to a new technology, customer base, or operational model? What are the success metrics? Cost savings, efficiency, gains, or market expansion.

iii) Conduct risk and feasibility analysis: In this segment, we see financial impact, asset cost, funding sources, potential return on investment, and operational challenges. We also identify how the pivot will impact existing infrastructure, workforce, and supply chains. Regulatory considerations ensure compliance with local, state, and federal guidelines.

iv) Follow a phase implementation plan: We implement a pilot program where we test new processes, technologies, or markets on a small scale before full adoption, incrementally roll out, gradually transition operations while maintaining existing services, trading, and change management, and ensure employers have the skills and knowledge to support the pivot. Then, we follow the next step of monitoring and adjusting the scale.

v) Track key metrics: We use the latest technologies like SCADA, IoT, and financial models to measure early performance.

vi) Adjust based on feedback: adapt based on real-world data and stakeholder input, scale strategically. Expand only after proving viability in smaller applications. For example, what major technology has been enhanced when we shift from traditional chlorination to UV disinfection? Municipal utilities facing strict disinfection by-product regulation need to pivot from chlorine-based treatment to UV treatment. So, regulatory pressure was there. We did pilot testing, financial modeling, gradual implementation, and full transit optimization. So, these are examples of the latest technology that has been developed.

In the early stages of my career, I received advice for adaptability: Don't wait until change is forced upon you. Innovate before it becomes a necessity. That is my key learning.

It matters more than people realize because many professional organizations resist change due to their comfort with existing processes.

However, waiting until new regulations, equipment failure, or market shifts occur for adoption can lead to higher costs, increased compliance requirements, risk, and operational inefficiencies. Being productive rather than reactive always smooths transactions, facilitates better financial planning, and provides a competitive edge in adapting to new technologies. Small incremental improvements in processes, technology, or workforce development make large-scale changes easier to implement when necessary.

During a major infrastructure upgrade at one of our key wastewater treatment plants, we encountered an unexpected regulatory change just weeks before a critical project milestone. New environmental guidelines required immediate adjustments to our treatment processes, changes that, under normal circumstances, would have meant a costly delay or a complete redesign of the project. I remember gathering our experts for an emergency meeting so we could start adopting and implementing a more flexible approach, supported by alternative technologies and operational adjustments. We all agreed that this would help the company meet deadlines while keeping us on established timelines.

Within 48 hours, we decided to integrate an advanced membrane filtration system, previously in its pilot phase, into our design. This decision was made on the spot, backed by real-time data and expert analysis. The swift pivot ensured compliance with the new regulations and resulted in a more energy-efficient and cost-effective operation than originally planned.

The outcome was remarkable:

- The plant was upgraded on schedule, preserving our client relationship and securing future contracts.

- The new system reduced energy consumption and maintenance costs, which will prove beneficial in the long run.

- The ability to adapt under pressure reinforced a culture of innovation and resilience within the team.

This experience taught me that the willingness to be flexible and make quick, informed decisions can transform potential setbacks into opportunities for innovation and success.

Future Trends Entrepreneurs Should Prepare For

The next generation of entrepreneurs, especially in our domain, needs a combination of technical expertise, adaptability, and strategic thinking to navigate early challenges. Therefore, mission-focused abilities, digital and technology proficiency, understanding AI, TOT, and automation for smarter business operations, using data analytics for decision-making, enhancing efficiency, gaining customer insights, and familiarity with cybersecurity to protect digital infrastructure is essential.

a. **Sustainability and environmental awareness:** integrating sustainable business practices into operations, navigating environmental regulations and compliance standards, innovating in water conservation, circular economics, climate resilience, problem-solving, and adaptability. We must be able to pilot strategies when market conditions change, learn quickly from failure, adjust accordingly, and stay ahead of disruptive trends and regulatory shifts.

b. **Financial and business acumen:** Strong financial literacy to manage cash flow, investments, and risks; the ability to develop scalable business models that balance profitability with impact; strategic planning for long-term growth and changing markets; communication leadership; building a strong network and partnerships with industry experts; leading diverse teams with collaborative leadership and a clear vision; and mastering storytelling and pitching to investors, customers, and stakeholders.

c. **Regulatory and policy understanding:** Staying ahead of compliance changes in an industry with strict regulation, and engaging with policymakers to influence industry direction. Entrepreneurs who blend innovation and sustainability leverage digital tools, stay agile, and have a great chance of succeeding.

So, that is my advice for the next generation of entrepreneurs.

Determining a new trend worth attention in our domain requires a balance of data-driven analysis, industry insight, and long-term feasibility assessment. We require a structured approach to achieve this and identify the driving forces behind the trend.

- Regulatory pressures: If a trend is linked to a new or upcoming regulation or single norm by government authorities, it's likely to have long-term importance.

- Market demand: Our utilities, government, or industrial investment area, growing demand suggests sustainability.

- Technology advancement: In the trend backed by scalable, proven technology, or is still experimental.

- Analyze adoption by industry leaders: Our major industry utilities, engineering firms, and technology providers are adopting this trend. Industry associations like the American and global water industries acknowledge their importance. Are competitors shifting their strategies towards it?

- Assess financial operational feasibility: Where we talk about cost versus benefit. Does that provide clear-cut saving efficiency gains, regulatory compliance benefits, or scalability?

Can it be implemented across different facility sizes and operation models?

Then we discuss the return on investment: Will it drive long-term value, or is it a short-term elude innovation?

- Test with pilot program or small-scale adoption: Running a controlled pilot test allows for real-world evaluation before we proceed with full-scale adoption. Gathering performance data helps validate whether a trend is practical or just high.

- Monitor longevity and industry consensus: A trend that persists for three years and gains widespread adoption or deeper investment. If a trend lacks long-term data or early adopters struggle with the implementation, it may not be sustainable. So, for example, if you're worth paying attention to, AI-driven leak detection has gained traction due to proven cost-saving efficiency improvement and scalability.

This is a less viable trend. Some experiments have struggled with desalination technologies due to their high cost and energy demand. So, these are the few examples we can take for this technology.

When there is validation of the long-term potential of a trend before investing, resource is a very critical parameter in water and wastewater for the industry, where regulatory changes, technological advancement, and infrastructure investment require careful planning. We follow a structural approach to this.

i. Market Analysis: We analyze market demand as government bodies, industries, or utilities actively invest in this area.

ii. Industry and peer benchmarking: Monitor early adopters, leading utilities, or private firms already implementing the technologies or practices.

iii. Cost-benefit and return on investment analysis: Technology or strategy should also consider financial sustainability over a 5 to 10-year horizon.

iv. Operational efficiency gains: Will it lead to measurable improvement in efficiency, compliance, or risk reduction?

v. Pilot testing and feasibility studies: We conduct small-scale trials and implement a solution in a limited capacity to assess major performance before we go for the large-scale full deployment.

vi. Gather real-world data: Use SCADA, IoT, or lab analysis to validate effectiveness.

vii. Expert and consultant research: We regularly engage with industry experts, consultants, and technology providers. We review scientific and technical studies, review previewed research, and examine case studies from similar projects, which gives us confidence.

viii. Scalability and adaptability: Once we have completed all this piloting, we will discuss it. We will discuss whether it can scale, whether the trend still requires viable infrastructure to grow, and whether it is a future growth. Since we are investing in it, technology should be a future, long-lasting, and sustainable improvement. Also, we will see whether it is integrated with upcoming digital tools, automation, or sustainability initiatives.

These are the few things we always consider.

The water and wastewater industry has undoubtedly evolved rapidly due to technological advancements as well as climate change. There are a number of things that can affect them currently:

a. Advanced treatment technologies: Regulation drives the adoption of advanced treatment technologies, such as activated carbon, ion exchange, and high-pressure membranes, to remove foreign chemicals and pharmaceuticals.

b. **Decentralized wastewater admittance:** Going for decentralized small systems for water and wastewater to cater to the easiest way of operation.

c. **Digital transformation as innovative management:** AI-driven detection, demand forecasting, and predictive maintenance to optimize the operations.

d. **SCADA and IoT expansion:** This includes real-time monitoring of water quality, pressure, and energy consumption to improve efficiency while also reducing downtime.

e. **Digital versions:** Virtual models of treatment plants and distribution networks to help operators simulate and optimize possible performances.

f. **Climate change resilience:** Given the crisis, utilities need to prepare for more frequent droughts, floods, and rising sea levels. This eventually means increased investment in stormwater management and infrastructure hardening.

g. **Strict regulatory and compliance enforcement:** The government is changing the discharge norms for drinking water and the filling standards. This requires upgrading to new technology; you can incorporate technology and business.

h. **Carbon footprint reduction:** The push for net-zero emissions will encourage utilities to adopt energy-efficient processes like energy digestion, biogas recovery, and renewable-powered treatment plants.

As we look ahead, several key trends are expected to define the business and economic landscape over the next ten years. These trends are driven by technological advancements, evolving consumer expectations, and global economic shifts: These trends indicate that the next decade will be characterized by rapid technological progress, an unwavering focus on sustainability, and an agile approach to business operations, all contributing to a dynamic and resilient global economy.

Key Reader Takeaways
- Innovation is necessary for business survival and long-term growth.

- Change is inevitable—embracing it is the key to long-term success.

- Technology can enhance efficiency, sustainability, and industry transformation.

- Creating a culture of innovation starts with leadership and team empowerment.

- Overcoming resistance to change requires strategic communication and gradual adoption.

- Continuous learning is the secret weapon of every successful entrepreneur.

The future belongs to leaders who embrace change and adapt proactively.

Start Your Innovation Journey Today
Reflection Exercise:
- Identify one outdated practice or system that needs to evolve in your business.

- Research one emerging technology that could improve efficiency or sustainability in your industry.

- Research one major trend in your industry and how you can incorporate it into your strategy.

- Create a plan for introducing a new process or tool within the next six months.

- Write down three steps you will take to become more adaptable in your leadership approach.

Share your innovation idea with a mentor, team, or industry expert and seek feedback on its feasibility.

Commit to learning something new: Attend a seminar, take an online course, or schedule a conversation with an industry leader to discuss upcoming trends.

Innovation is the difference between staying relevant and becoming obsolete. But while technology and processes are vital, true success isn't just about business; it's about creating impact. The only way to future-proof your business is to embrace change, adapt quickly, and keep learning. But adaptability alone isn't enough; you also need a clear roadmap to guide your entrepreneurial journey. In the next chapter, we'll explore how entrepreneurs can move beyond profits to build a lasting legacy that contributes to society.

8

Creating a Lasting Impact Beyond Business Success

⊶•–•■•–•■•–•■•–•■•–•❮❮❯❯•–•■•–•■•–•■•–•■•–•⊷

I magine standing at the peak of your career, looking back at everything you've built. What would matter the most—your revenue figures, the number of deals closed, or your impact on the world? Business success is temporary, but a true legacy is built through the lives you touch, the communities you uplift, and the values you pass on.

Many entrepreneurs focus on growth, wealth, and expansion, but the most enduring businesses create value beyond financial success.

Business was never just about profits—it was about creating solutions that benefit society, mentoring the next generation, and contributing to long-term sustainability. In this chapter, we explore how entrepreneurs can move beyond financial achievements to leave a meaningful legacy. It is meant to guide you through building a lasting impact through mentorship, social responsibility, and ethical leadership.

The Shift from Success to Significance

Every business starts with the intention of making mega profits and getting those "big bucks." However, as companies grow, a few face crises like backlash, employee dissatisfaction, or ethical scandals, forcing them to rethink their priorities in life. In our business, we know that water is critical for human life. So, when we consider a country like India, which has the largest population globally, approximately 25% of its population resides there.

Yet, around 34% of people in India do not have access to drinkable water. In this way, we connect and see that profit is not the only focus in our business; we emphasize how we can change people's lives through water treatment, making it drinkable, recycling, and preserving it.

In our generation, we see the transition from river to dam, dam to tap, tap to bottle. It will be in a capsule if we do not take care of this vital element. What we manage to give to our next generation is the most important from a business perspective. We strive to work in this public domain, where we can truly impact people's lives by providing water, which is essential for saving human lives.

During a crisis like the pandemic, the whole world is shut down, but people still risked their lives for water. The whole world was limited to inside their houses, but we were in the field and provided them with water to show that we worked to give them happiness. We wanted to add value to people's lives.

In situations like the pandemic, when you go to rural areas, you see people unable to get water in the summer. In cities like Pune and Bangalore, where water scarcity is a problem, people leave their homes because no water is available. So that kind of crisis we've seen gives us more power to work in this field and make people's lives easier.

When the idea of "leaving a legacy" really comes up, it isn't just about making a name for yourself. In its roots, it means creating something meaningful that outlasts you, whether it is your idea, impact, or positive change in people's lives. It is more than just success; it's about the significance you create.

We frequently discuss how to optimally preserve water and reduce losses through effective networking, automation, and the implementation of new technologies. For instance, we recycled 200 million liters of water daily through a project executed in a city in Maharashtra. The 200 million liters of water saved each day benefit approximately 10-15 lakh individuals. If we can maintain this for 365 days a year, we could extend that water supply during summer for up to two months; in case of drought, people can survive with the recycled water. Our efforts not only help people access water but also teach others how they can contribute to this process as regular individuals. That is the legacy we aim to create.

People have started to talk about water preservation, recycling, and zero liquid discharge. In a way, they see this as a brand where we can really impact people's lives. They should look upon us as people who can help them survive to the next generation through this work in our domain.

Measuring long-term impact on financial success means looking at your work's deeper, lasting effect on people, communities, and the world. It's also about people's growth and well-being. Have you helped others improve their lives or career mindsets? This could have been through mentorship, leadership, or community-building.

Additionally, making contributions to long-term positive change, whether in environmental sustainability, ethical business practices, or social progress, is equally important. The company places a strong emphasis on sustainability and its ethical practices in this area.

To provide ongoing help and support in the industry, innovative ideas that endure are essential. Even when projects or solutions become obsolete, ideas, products, and contributions can remain useful and relevant for years to come. If people are going to refer to those ideas in the long term, they will have a lasting impact on people's lives.

When the culture or industry shifts, we try to change the way we operate. This includes changing people's thinking about our project or domain, which often inspires new approaches.

The other thing that people are required to keep in mind is legacy in relationships and reputation: the way we do ethical business, and legacy. We are creating this legacy by preserving, reducing, and recycling. That gives the trust because we have been together for years, and we are able to do it on a consistent and sustainable basis. People are looking at us as leaders in that segment. These are the few things I can share for the long-term impact beyond financials.

When attending the GWI, Global Water Intelligence, we discuss how much water we are treating, how much we recycle, and how many people have access to drinkable water. Thus, the rating depends on the amenity index. In my last two entrepreneurial ventures, two organizations have ranked among the top 50 companies providing such services. Therefore, this assessment goes beyond financials; it relies on the humanity index.

Mentoring the Next Generation

People have been working with me for a long time, and they have become key players in many of the ideas and proposals we work on. It is teamwork; every individual contributes to that success. Many people are not working with me currently, but have witnessed my leadership style nonetheless. Now they're leading some water company, and that gives immense pleasure when we see somebody working with you, and now he's adding some growth to the industry and legacy, and what learnings they have taken from the team, and they're carrying forward.

I mentored somebody who had come from a very small company as a proposal engineer, and he worked with me for around six or seven years. He was given a lot of freedom and made many mistakes, but there was always a clear intent to learn. So, he always crossed those boundaries beyond the work environment, consistently striving to add value, and now he's heading one of the water companies. I managed to watch his transition from training proposal engineer to heading a water company in just 10 years. That's the kind of person who serves as the best kind of example, and there are many more people like that.

Dedication, passion, understanding, and work beyond the boundaries give them more exposure.

One core value I instill in mentorship is long-term thinking, which I believe is the most important skill. Whether it is business, leadership, or personal growth, I encourage people to make decisions that aren't just about immediate gains but more geared towards long-lasting impact. That means prioritizing integrity over structures, relationships over transactions, and sustainable growth over quick wins. It is about building something meaningful that stands the test of time. That is the most important, and I always emphasize this. Short-term gains aren't as critical and vital to a company, especially compared to the long-lasting impact one tries to make. This is a core value as a mentor, and we can build it into our mentorship.

In India, around 90% of startups wind up in a few years, one or two years. So why is it happening? Because people want everything overnight. As an entrepreneur, any mission and vision typically cannot be short-term. You have to give it at least five years to build a journey there. Today, a lot of people don't have that kind of patience.

That's why we should think long-term and be strategic planners. The strategy should be in place, and there should always be long-term strategic planning. That is going to last long. Otherwise, no successful enterprises or entrepreneurs can be created overnight. It's a process.

The most important quality in a future leader is vision with integrity.

A leader needs to be someone who can see the bigger picture, inspire others, and make bold decisions, while staying grounded in strong values is the most important thing for me.

A great leader doesn't focus on profit but understands the long-term impact of their choices on employees, customers, and the world. They need resilience to navigate challenges, emotional intelligence to build strong relationships, and humanity to keep learning. So, the most impactful thing in leadership is vision with integrity.

A few years ago, I had the opportunity to mentor a young engineer who had just joined our water treatment company. Though technically skilled, he struggled with confidence, leadership, and decision-making—essential traits for growth in the industry.

During his initial months, he hesitated to speak up in meetings and often doubted his recommendations. I noticed his technical expertise, but also saw that he needed guidance to step into a leadership role. So here were some measures I undertook:

- **One-on-One Coaching** – I scheduled weekly discussions where we worked on problem-solving, confidence-building, and strategic thinking.

- **Exposure to Bigger Challenges** – I encouraged him to lead a small team in optimizing an outdated wastewater treatment process.

- **Encouraging Independent Decision-Making** – I challenged him to analyze issues and propose recommendations instead of providing solutions.

Within a year, he went from being a hesitant engineer to leading a crucial water conservation project for the company. His project resulted in:

- A 20% reduction in water losses through system optimization.

- Recognition from senior leadership, leading to a fast-track promotion.

- Increased confidence, allowing him to mentor junior engineers.

Mentoring isn't just about teaching technical skills—it's about instilling confidence, empowering decision-making, and creating future leaders. Seeing him grow into a leadership role reaffirmed my belief that investing time in people is one of the best long-term strategies for success.

Securing the Future of Your Business and Society

Balancing profitability with social contributions comes down to the integrity of the business's core purpose rather than treating it as an afterthought. Balancing is the most important thing. The key way to achieve success is to have balance, which is the most important.

i) Align purpose with profit: The best businesses solve real problems to benefit both people and the bottom line. Take sustainability, or terms like social impact. If you align your purpose with profit, then it is a balance.

ii) Sustainable growth over short-term gains: Making ethical long-term decisions often leads to more resilient success, and avoiding exploitative work builds trust and loyalty with customers and employees.

iii) Invest in the people: People are the asset for the organization. You have to create a culture where people can share their thoughts and ideas, recognize their aspirations, and how you can assist them to fuel a better performance from them. You can gain their trust, and that is converted to loyalty. They can single-handedly sustain you for the long term.

iv) Use profits as a tool for impact: Profitability allows social good companies that prioritize both aspects to demonstrate that businesses can be compelled to change.

When we talk about generational wealth, we must not get too caught up in the value of money but rather focus on mindset and principles. The next generation's adaptability and financial literacy can sustain and grow; they should be inherent.

We have to share our experience, knowledge, continuous learning, and insight to help them navigate life and business. So, educational knowledge is also an important factor.

The reputation and legacy we carry, the brand, should be respected for integrity influence, and opening doors. If we create a brand that can have an impact when people see the value, so that next-generation doors can be opened for them, that legacy should be carried.

It's vital to strike a balance between profitability and running the business. You also need to balance the short term and the long term.

Balancing business success with social contribution is exemplified by entrepreneurs in the water and wastewater industry. Notable figures include:

1. Yvette Ishimwe – Founder and CEO of Iriba Water Group

Yvette Ishimwe, a Rwandan entrepreneur, founded Iriba Water Group in 2017 to combat water scarcity in underserved communities. The company runs water kiosks and filtration systems, offering affordable and safe drinking water. By 2023, Iriba's 74 Tap & Drink systems will have served over 300,000 individuals in Rwanda and the Democratic Republic of Congo, generated 68 jobs, and lowered CO_2 emissions by 62 metric tons monthly.

2. Abhishek Nath – Founder of LooCafe

Indian entrepreneur Abhishek Nath launched LooCafe in 2018 to transform public sanitation. LooCafe provides prefabricated, complimentary public restrooms paired with cafés, improving urban sanitation and generating job opportunities. By 2023, LooCafe aims to have set up more than 400 facilities throughout India, making substantial contributions to the country's sanitation infrastructure.

3. Daigo Ishiyama – Chief Engineer of SATO

In 2012, Daigo Ishiyama spearheaded the creation of the SATO pan, a groundbreaking and cost-effective toilet solution tailored for low-income countries. This design requires minimal water and enhances hygiene by blocking insects and odors. By 2024, over 800,000 units were installed in its inaugural year, and the product has expanded to 45 countries, benefiting more than 68 million individuals with improved sanitation.

These entrepreneurs demonstrate that integrating social responsibility with business objectives can lead to sustainable success and substantial community benefits.

Making Business a Force for Good

The domain we are in is related to human life. There are many villages where we take Corporate Social Responsibility (CSR) and deal with the processes there. There are small hill towns, and we help them so they can pull the water from there. We have also set up some packaged systems where they can treat the unclean water and provide drinkable water. We participate in that kind of social awareness, and there are a few towns where we identify, and every year we work with those villages to make them aware of the water pollution, the drinking water, and how it can be safe. Every year, we take that initiative to exercise our CSR to the best of our abilities. We have a social impact on the community. Running a common Effluent Treatment Plant, we treat the water as much as necessary to be recycled.

We even provide water treatment packages for rural areas. Altogether, we are extremely aware of the role we play and try our best to live up to it every day. Now, there is a lot of focus on water and wastewater because, looking at water scarcity, hardly any drinkable water is available to less than one percent of the population. Most of the plants are more than 30 to 40 years old. So, there is a massive need for infrastructure development and rehabilitation, especially with huge crowds of people shifting from rural to urban areas.

Urban infrastructure is under a lot of load, and it cannot support the growth that is coming. So, it is challenging when people just put the borewell and take the groundwater. It will take a few hundred years to get back to that water limit, and the increasing temperatures due to global warming will also facilitate the temperature rise.

The temperature is almost 50 degrees in some parts of India. There is pollution and uneven rain. There have been huge impacts on the weather and climate of the country, and the effects may be disastrous in many ways. So, as a company, we feel the government should focus more on this, and people should be aware of our environmental impact. Everyone has to take this responsibility in their own way, and maybe plans can be made to decide how to contribute to protecting a sustainable environment, building sustainable solutions, and preserving this vital element on the earth.

Initiatives:

The biggest things we can discuss are the three R's: reduce, reuse, and recycle. We were already using this kind of framework. We also executed a few projects in my past entrepreneurship. We executed one of India's most significant recycled projects, saving a huge volume of wastewater. Now, it has become a policy for the government to require any industry in the surrounding area to have a sewage treatment plant.

They have to go for the recycling of sewage water. We save fresh water, which is made drinkable. So, we feel like we have had some impact on people's lives.

We are focusing on recycling water. Therefore, we discuss this with the government authorities. In the city, there is a sewage plant. You provide the sewage, and we will treat it; then, you will make it compulsory to use it for construction, gardening, cleaning, and other processes where it can be conserved. There are several projects where the government is partnering with other entities to reuse this sewage water for these purposes. This way, we can save fresh water, significantly impacting human life.

Whatever vision and mission we have, we are in the right place and have so many years of experience. This is a business that has a social impact. Actually, our goal is not only about profit, but also about the socio-economic impact we will make. And whatever business domain we are in, I believe we can preserve this vital element on the earth, and we are making a profit and a social impact. We upgrade ourselves with new technologies and raising more awareness. You might find a vision with different steps, but we are steadily moving along with our vision.

Sustainability has become a core business priority for companies in the water and infrastructure sectors as they respond to climate change, water scarcity, and regulatory pressures. Leading organizations are adopting innovative strategies to ensure long-term resource efficiency, environmental protection, and financial viability.

•   **Circular Water Management:** Companies are transitioning from a linear "use-and-dispose" framework to a circular water economy, emphasizing water recycling, reuse, and repurposing.

Xylem Inc. has created sophisticated smart water solutions that identify leaks, optimize water usage, and reduce wastewater emissions.

This reduces freshwater consumption and promotes long-term sustainability.

• **Green Infrastructure & Nature-Based Solutions:** Sustainable urban planning now integrates nature-based solutions into water management, aiming to mitigate flooding, enhance water quality, and boost biodiversity.

Singapore's ABC Waters Program turns urban waterways into environmentally friendly areas that effectively manage stormwater. This reduces urban flooding and improves groundwater replenishment.

• **Energy Efficiency in Water Treatment:** Water treatment facilities consume a significant amount of energy. Companies are investing in eco-friendly technologies and renewable energy to lessen their carbon footprint.

Veolia has installed biogas recovery systems in wastewater treatment plants, using organic waste to produce energy. This lowers operational costs and carbon emissions, creating a sustainable energy cycle.

• **Smart Water Technologies & AI Integration:** The application of digital twins, IoT sensors, and AI-driven analytics enables companies to monitor water systems in real-time and maximize resource efficiency.

Suez utilizes AI-enhanced water quality monitoring to mitigate contamination risks and improve efficiency. This curtails water losses, boosts service delivery, and reduces operational expenses.

• **Sustainable Infrastructure & Climate Resilience:** The rise in extreme weather events emphasizes the importance of climate-resilient infrastructure that can withstand droughts, floods, and rising sea levels. Barwon Water's alternative water grid in Australia repurposes wastewater and stormwater for agricultural and industrial use. This strengthens water security while decreasing reliance on freshwater sources.

Companies in the water and infrastructure sectors are proving that sustainability is both a responsibility and a business advantage. By embracing innovation, circular water practices, and smart technologies, these organizations build resilience, reduce costs, and secure long-term success in a water-scarce world.

How to Ensure Your Work Continues Beyond You

Legacy is what we are going to leave, which will impact people's lives. Already, the transition we talk about, from river to capsule, and by adding this from treatment to recycling to reuse, we are taking the step that will last forever. People will probably always remember us for the legacy that we create and for preserving this vitality.

Two opinions are taken into consideration for your reputation: one is the industry and the other is the general public, because we are in the government adjacent sector. When we take the contract from some other company, and we see people talking about the water quality, they don't understand the technical aspects. Still, they see the water's clarity and test the water, and they feel pleased. We feel happy when a common man talks about what he observed for so many years, and now, after seeing or drinking this water, what we feel gives us more happiness.

As a government, they see that this company is really impacting life. The way we maintain the plant, they see improvement, the infrastructure, and an investment in life. So, it is also an indirect way of saving their wealth. It is public property. It is our wealth, and if we can preserve the wealth of the plant by maintaining it properly, it reduces the cost, and we are able to reduce the waste and power. If we reduce the power, we have thermal power, and when we create thermal power, there is a lot of pollution. So when we talk about the impact on carbon credits, they can also opt for the carbon credit.

People always see that kind of value chain we are creating in this company, creating a value chain that impacts humans and the environment, and converts it into wealth.

I always believe in the system. The organization should not run on a person but on the system. I always try to create a system first. We have granted that rigid system, and we are very clear with our vision and mission. If we step away today, I think 20, 25, and 30 years of legacy should be carried because the platform we created and the company can see the growth will be there and add value to human life. So, we are already able to make that kind of structure.

My vision is that we always say no water, no life, no blue, no green, so I want this idea to be carried. People should talk about reducing, recycling, and reusing; these are the future beliefs that should be maintained. I want to leave these three things that people carry and work upon with new technology, new ideas, and new strategies, and I believe we have to give the environment to the next generation. We discuss a sustainable environment and the basic need for water to be drinkable for the next generation.

One of the biggest blind spots, I think, regarding the legacy is thinking about it later, as if legacy is something you are behind after reaching financial success, rather than something shaped by daily decisions. Many people just talk about the growth, profit, and scaling up, and they don't realize their culture, values, and impact are already forming their legacy in real time. People talk about only short-term profits, which don't show the organizational culture and long-term rate. So that is a blind spot that I can see.

So people should always talk about this long-term strategy because vision and missions are not short-term, in my view. It is a long-term process. In our kind of system, we talk about employees as our asset because we are human and customer-centric, and the common people, because we are dealing with drinking water as wastewater treatment.

So it will impact people's lives. When we make any decision, think about this ecosystem, how we are dealing with it, and how we are going to value it. The biggest blind spots are short-term profit. They ignore the other integrity values. So people are making compromises on those things.

A leader's legacy is not just about the projects completed or the revenue generated—it's about the impact left behind on people, communities, and the industry itself.

1. **Transforming Water Accessibility & Sustainability**

a. A lasting legacy would be one where clean, sustainable water solutions become the norm, not a challenge.

b. Ensuring that future generations inherit a world where water scarcity is minimized through innovation and responsible management.

2. **Championing Innovation & Smart Water Management**

a. The future of water lies in digital solutions, AI-driven efficiency, and circular economy principles.

b. A leader's vision should focus on integrating technology into water infrastructure to make systems more efficient, predictive, and resilient.

3. **Building a Culture of Leadership & Mentorship**

a. Beyond infrastructure, a true legacy is built through people, developing the next generation of water leaders who will continue the mission.

b. Investing in education, mentorship, and workforce development ensures that expertise is passed down and expanded.

4. **Advocating for Policy & Global Water Resilience**

a. A leader's impact is amplified by shaping policies and industry standards that prioritize sustainability and long-term resilience.

b. Working with governments, regulators, and global organizations to drive change on a systemic level.

A legacy in the water and infrastructure industry should not just be measured in projects built but in lives improved, environments restored, and innovations pioneered. The true mark of leadership is when the work continues to make a difference even decades later.

Key Reader Takeaways

- True success comes from creating a lasting impact, not just making money.

- Mentorship and knowledge-sharing shape future generations of leaders.

- Strong financial management enables both business growth and social responsibility.

- Sustainability and ethical leadership are key to long-term influence.

- Leaving a legacy requires intentional planning and purpose-driven leadership.

Start Building Your Legacy Today
Reflection Exercise:

- Define what impact means to you beyond financial success.

- Identify one area where you can mentor or give back in your industry.

- Write a personal vision statement for the legacy you want to leave behind.

Take one step today—whether it's mentoring someone, starting a community initiative, or integrating sustainability into your business strategy.

Success is temporary, but impact is permanent. The entrepreneurs who leave the greatest legacies are those who build beyond themselves. But you must adapt to a rapidly changing world to ensure the impact lasts.

In the final chapter, we'll combine everything with a structured action plan to turn these lessons into a powerful, long-term business strategy.

9

Your Roadmap to Entrepreneurial Success – A Step-by-Step Guide

································《◇》································

I magine standing at the edge of a vast landscape, the horizon stretching out in every direction. You have a map in hand, but the choices are yours to make. You could go to the left, right, or straight ahead. Every step becomes your journey to a new place, defining your path. This is where true entrepreneurship begins—not in dreaming but executing with clarity, purpose, and strategy.

Throughout this book, we have discussed hard-earned lessons, leadership insights, and real-world strategies to help you navigate the entrepreneurial journey. Now, it's time to combine everything into a clear, actionable roadmap that turns knowledge into results.

Many aspiring entrepreneurs read, research, and dream, but only a few take decisive action. The difference between those who succeed and those who don't lies in execution. This chapter provides a step-by-step roadmap to help readers apply the lessons learned in this book to their own businesses and careers.

Clarity of Purpose – Start with Your 'Why'

The core purpose of our business is to ensure public health, environmental protection, and operational reliability. However, there will always be moments when this vision or mission is truly tested.

For example, when responding to a major contamination event, a significant challenge is the wastewater treatment plan, specifically detecting high levels of industrial contamination in the effluent, which can threaten to overwhelm the system and lead to permit violations. Since government authorities have established norms for discharging the affiliate, if not addressed promptly, this could have led to various consequences, primarily a public health risk from potential drinking water contamination, environmental damage due to untreated discharge, regulatory fines, and legal repercussions. These are the few immediate, impactful things that will happen.

Then, there was the test of purpose. The team had to decide whether to immediately shut down the affected intake, potentially disrupting services for thousands of people, or find an alternative treatment solution in real time. Therefore, engineers and operators had to collaborate immediately, leveraging advanced treatment methods, temporary solutions for contaminants, and expedited regulatory approvals.

After taking those steps, we got a combination of chemical treatment adjustments and a temporary storage solution to help manage the contamination without shutting down services. Investigation identifies the source of contaminants and industrial facilities violating discharge permits, which led to improved monitoring and enforcement. The crisis reinforced the need for real-time monitoring, emergency preparedness, and stronger partnerships with local industries.

So, what is our key takeaway after dealing with this? This moment tests our core mission, balancing operational, regulatory, and public health responsibilities under pressure. The experience led to permanent process improvement that is trending toward long-term resilience. So, these are the things that I can see. My perspective is toward a moment where our core purpose is truly tested.

After facing a major contamination event or any critical challenge in the industry, realigning with core purpose requires immediate corrective action and long-term systematic improvements. So, some innovations are heavily discussed.

The process we follow and the steps we learn from this crisis management are:

- Reflect and respond by conducting a root cause analysis to identify the issues.

- Collaborate with operators, engineers, regulators, and impacted stakeholders to collect insights.

- Enact emergency measures to avoid purpose contamination while maintaining compliance.

Then, the second stage arises, where we discuss strengthening preventive measures.

- Upgrade the real-time monitoring system to detect contaminants earlier.

- Improve enforcement of industrial pretreatment to hold violators accountable.

- Develop quicker response protocols for future emergencies.

And finally, we reach the third step, which is reinforcing team alignment and training.

- Conduct a post-incident debrief to discuss lessons, learn, and ensure alignment with the mission.

- Provide targeted training on emergency response, crisis management, and regulatory compliance.

- Strengthen collaboration with local industries to prevent future issues.

In an attempt to pursue long-term cultural changes, we consciously chose to shift from reactive to more proactive upgrades by investing in predictive analytics. We have had several internal talks about AI-driven monitoring and resilience planning. This also helped encourage a continuous learning culture, ensuring past mistakes lead to smart future decisions.

Using the crisis as a defining moment to reinforce why the team would directly impact public health, environment, safety, and operational excellence will always be a good move. Re-aligning with the core purpose isn't just about fixing the immediate issue. It's about using the challenges to drive lasting improvement, strengthen accountability, and reform commitment to public trust.

The most important thing is communication with stakeholders. Engage with public regulators and leadership teams to rebuild our trust. Share a transparency report detailing the response, corrective action, and long-term improvements. Use the incident to advocate for infrastructure upgrades or policy changes.

The second most important mindset shift for an aspiring entrepreneur is to embrace adaptability. Adaptability allows you to recognize that failure, feedback, and rapid change are not setbacks but essential components of growth.

When you shift your perspective to see every challenge as an opportunity to learn and build resilience and the agility needed to navigate uncertainty, a proactive, interactive approach empowers you to pivot quickly, innovate continuously, and succeed in every volume market.

There was a moment when a company decided to integrate its personal commitment to environmental stewardship directly into the business model. The leadership had long believed this industry was meant to be about compliance and efficiency, giving back to the community, and protecting the environment. We talked about the water utility facing the challenges of aging infrastructure, rising operational costs, and deciding to invest in a green infrastructure initiative. Instead of solely focusing on short-term fixes, there was a defining shift to be committed to upgrading the treatment processes and sustainable energy, energy-efficient technologies, and integrating water use, where we talk about reduced recycling and reuse, strategies that reduce overall water consumption.

If we align this scenario with our core values:

- **Environmental responsibility:** Another factor driving these initiatives is the company's commitment to reducing its environmental footprint and maintaining environmental consciousness.

- **Community focus:** They aim to improve water quality and ensure local communities have access to a reliable water supply, thereby supporting the livelihoods and community health of residents.

- **Long-term thinking:** Rather than pursuing quick fixes, we prioritize long-term benefits and sustainability.

- **The unexpected success:** Overall cost savings over time from sustainable upgrades have resulted in energy savings and lower maintenance costs. This speaks to the company's proactive stances, which have managed to attract positive media attention and boost community trust.

Taking those steps gives a market differentiation. By aligning business models with deeply held personal and corporate values, we achieve operational efficiency and position ourselves as industrial leaders in sustainability. This experience reinforces the idea that when you integrate your personal values into the business strategy, you are more likely to create a resilient, forward-thinking organization that can capitalize on unexpected opportunities.

In one industry, the customer has built a plant, and a competitor builds for the buyer. They are talking about zero liquid discharge, a petrochemical kind of plant. Still, technology cannot take that industrial effluent with a characteristic and cannot do a zero liquid discharge.

It is challenging for them to dispose of that effluent, looking at the government norms for that isolation. So, our team has put a lot of effort into some piloting, and we have improved the processes. By improving the processes we can take that effluent into the plant because we are the operator of this plant and by our technology excellence we able to treat the effluent by improving some processes and adding some equipment into it and customer can make that plant as a zero liquid discharge plant and finally they solve the problems.

In order to really drive these points home, people tend to come up with personal mission statements. Creating a personal mission statement starts with deep self-reflection. Use this tool to assess your values, strengths, passions, and goals, and then craft a statement that aligns with who you are and what you aspire to achieve.

Step 1: Reflect on Your Core Values

List Your Top 5 Values, qualities, or principles that are non-negotiable in your life (e.g., integrity, innovation, compassion, sustainability, excellence). Which values make me feel most fulfilled and authentic?

Step 2: Identify Your Passions and Interests

Identify activities that energize you. Think about what you enjoy doing, whether it's solving complex problems or mentoring others. When do you feel most inspired and engaged?

Step 3: Assess Your Strengths and Skills

You can perform a SWOT Analysis. Figure out your strengths, weaknesses, opportunities, and threats. In what ways can you address or overcome my weaknesses?

Step 4: Define Your Long-Term Goals

Set clear, measurable goals, maybe consider where you want to be in 5, 10, or 20 years, both in your career and personal life.

Step 5: Craft Your Personal Mission Statement

Then you can use the information from the previous steps to write a statement that combines your purpose, values, and goals.

Step 6: Review and Refine

Make sure to gather feedback from those around you, ensure your missions and goals are honest and aligned with your ideals, and periodically revisit all the details to check whether anything has changed or needs to be corrected.

The Power of Strategic Goal Setting

It's always beneficial to have two modes of planning. The first one set in place for us is the immediate plan, an annual business plan. One is strategic planning. Breaking long-term goals into smaller, manageable steps is a powerful strategy to ensure steady progress and maintain momentum. I will explain a few steps and how they can help.

i. Specify and articulate clearly what kind of success we are looking for and identify measurable outcomes. Things like reducing product costs, improving efficiency, and improving customer satisfaction.

ii. Then, we break our long-term goal into phases or milestones. For example, if you are rolling out new water treatment technology, some phases might include pilot testing, regulatory approvals, and full-scale deployment. Then, we discuss possible timelines, setting tentative deadlines for each phase to create a sense of urgency and allow things to fall into place quickly.

iii. The next step is creating actionable tasks and specific actions to complete the job. We break down each phase and list the specific tasks that make it up. Then we assign responsibility to ensure each task has a clear owner and defined outcomes. Prioritize, focusing on tasks that have the greatest impact or are present for subsequent steps.

iv. We discuss monitoring progress and adjusting, where we see regular checkups and set weekly or monthly reviews to assess progress. We use real-time data from a system like SCADA or a project management tool to adjust plans. A program, no matter how small, can motivate the team.

v. We discuss more ways to stay aligned and adaptive. We record any improvements as progress, learn from each phase, and incorporate the notes on our approach.

Breaking our long-term goal into smaller, actionable steps makes the journey more manageable and provides frequent checkpoints to validate whether we are on the right path.

One example that comes to mind when considering this question is the goal of transferring a traditional wet water treatment plan into a digitally enabled predictive maintenance operation. Due to its scale and complexity, this project initially seemed daunting, so we systematically broke it down into steps.

We defined the overall goal. Then, we chose to transition reactive time-based maintenance to a productive maintenance system using digital tools. Third, we discussed the outcome: improving equipment reliability, reducing downtime, and optimizing maintenance costs.

The step after that is to conduct a comprehensive assessment involving a baseline evaluation, a review of the current maintenance record, and a failure platform for equipment performance data. Then, we did the technology research available on sensors, SCADA integrators, and AI analytics platforms suitable for our specific assets.

Then, in the next step, we encourage a breakdown into manageable sizes. In the first phase, we did some pilot programming. Again, we passed through a few steps in pilot programming, such as selection. Choose one critical subsystem for initial testing. Then we talk about implementation. Installed IoT sensors and set up a SCADA interface to collect real-time data.

Then comes testing. We ran the system for several months to gather performance data and validate the predictive model. Then we evaluated and iterated, using data analytics to analyze sensor data to identify early warning signs of equipment failure.

Then, the feedback loop, where maintenance is adjusted, should be based on predictive insight, and the algorithm should be fine-tuned as necessary.

Next: scaling up, a gradual rollout that extends the technology to additional critical assets, using lessons learned from the pilot to streamline deployment.

Full integration: the predictive maintenance system with the existing maintenance management process for ongoing monitoring and continuous improvement.

We monitor, adapt, and optimize. So, regular reviews and monthly checkups are set up to review system performance and make necessary adjustments.

Continuous improvement is the innovation we talk about. We use real-world feedback to refine both the technology and maintenance protocols. The insurance system is adapted to present research.

These are the steps we follow. What is the outcome of this? By breaking the overall main goal into a pilot phase, iterative evaluation, and gradually scaling the project, not only does it become manageable, but it ultimately leads to a significant reduction of unplanned downtime and maintenance calls. It also improves overall confidence in transitioning to a more proactive maintenance culture. So, these are the examples I can share and the steps we follow.

The goal is to transfer a traditional wastewater replacement plant into a digitally enabled predictive maintenance operation. We are following a traditional plant that we want to upgrade with a digital monitoring system.

A story about how small, strategic steps led to a significant breakthrough in his career.

A Resilient Business Plan – Execution Over Perfection

A common misconception in execution is that it is straightforward. As you can see, it is a linear process where you simply follow a well-lit plan to success. Many entrepreneurs believe that success will naturally follow once the idea of strategy is in place. However, in reality, execution is a dynamic factor. It is an iterative process that involves continuous adoption.

Plans rarely unfold exactly as expected. Real-world conditions demand constant monitoring and adjustment; sometimes, you have radical views.

Even the best ideas require a robust system, effective team coordination, discipline, and project management to overcome unforeseen challenges. Execution is about testing, gathering feedback, and refining your approach. It requires a willingness to learn from failures and adapt quickly. The essence of execution is not just having a great idea. Despite setbacks and evolving circumstances, it is about the persistent effort to translate that idea into reality.

Execution is an art. It is not a science. It's not just that you have a clear idea and, through planning, you execute it. There are many challenges we face when implementing any idea. We must accept and adopt those challenges and see how the process can be improved to achieve the desired result by enhancing this process.

In my view, many successful entrepreneurs in the water and wastewater management industry and beyond, consistent daily routines play a pivotal role in managing clarity, focus, and adaptability. Here, I want to share some habits proven to be particularly impactful.

I usually follow morning strategic planning. Starting the day with a review of key priorities helps ensure that both short-term tasks and long-term projects stay on track. This might include reviewing performance metrics, industry news, or upcoming regulatory changes.

Second, continuous learning. Dedicating time daily to reading industry publications, listening to podcasts, or attending brief webinars gives us a broad understanding of emerging trends and technologies. Staying informed is crucial in an industry with constant regulatory and technological changes.

After that comes data-driven decision reviews, incorporating a daily routine to analyze operational data or financial performance can help catch issues early and allow for quick pivots. This habit is the issue of decision-making being grounded in real-time insights.

I also made it a conscious point to practice reflection and journaling. Taking a few minutes at the end of the day to reflect on what worked well and what could be improved fosters a mindset of continuous improvement, often leading to more innovative problem-solving.

The most important thing is regular communication. Engaging with team members and industry peers daily through quick check-ins, email updates, or collaborative platforms helps maintain alignment and ensure that everyone is focused on the organization's core mission.

These daily habits create a framework that keeps operations running smoothly and builds resilience and adaptability, which are essential for long-term success. So, these are the routines that I feel are helpful for us to focus on.

The most significant action I can take today is to identify and launch a high-impact pilot project that aligns with our strategic prioritization. Any technological upgradation? If you are an innovative company, you should focus on not being high-risk. You go for the calculated risk, where we talk about piloting. With a small-scale system, we can pilot our ideas and make them successful. Then we can shift to the large scale, where the risks get reduced and the confidence increases when we do the piloting. So, my advice is, don't rush for the bigger thing. It's a start. Start with small steps, successfully pilot, and then launch on the biggest scale.

For example, if you are considering starting a pilot for productive maintenance using IoT sensors and data analytics. This approach allows us to test new technologies on a smaller scale, validate their benefits, and build momentum for large-scale implementation without overwhelming our current operations.

Focusing on well-defined, manageable projects that directly address key operational challenges, such as reducing unplanned downtime or improving compliance, can yield immediate improvement and create a proof of concept that can inform and accelerate future investment.

Setting and tracking long-term business goals involves a systematic approach that connects my vision to daily operations while remaining flexible enough to adjust to changes.

The strategy that my organization uses, which I can see, defines a clear vision and sets specific goals. When we talk about the vision-mission, the vision statement starts with a clear understanding of where we want our business to be in the long term.

Then, when discussing the SMART goals, we ensure each goal is specific, measurable, achievable, relevant, and time-bound. For example, we are upgrading treatment plant technology when discussing reducing energy cost by 20% in 5 years. So, that is the SMART where we identify specific goals, measure them, achieve them, and ensure they are relevant to our industry.

We also discuss breaking goals into manageable milestones, piloting with phase implementation, and dividing long-term goals into short-term phases. We also discuss quarterly, monthly, and annually with distinct milestones.

In the third step, we discuss using data and key performance indicators (KPIs). Establishing a matrix, we identify the KPIs that best reflect progress towards our goals, such as operational efficiency, regulatory compliance, or customer satisfaction.

The fourth one is about regular reviews and adjustments. Periodic check-ins should be reviewed regularly, monthly, or quarterly to assess progress, discuss challenges, and make necessary adjustments.

Additionally, we use feedback loops from these reviews to refine strategies and adapt to new market or regulatory changes. Then, engage and communicate with a team through transparent communication. Keep our team informed about the long-term vision and how their work contributes to goals.

It's also incredibly important to encourage cross-functional collaboration to ensure all parts of the organization are aligned and moving in the same direction.

We can keep our business on track and aligned in an ever-changing industry landscape by breaking long-term goals into actionable steps, monitoring progress with measurable indicators, and maintaining open communication.

Our team was grappling with recurring pump failures in one of the wastewater treatment plants in western India. We had heard about a few sensor-based monitoring technologies that promised early detection of equipment issues. Although we haven't completed all the technical evaluations or secured a perfect integration plan, we launched a small-scale pilot project, essentially starting before we felt entirely ready.

So, what happened by implementing these steps? Early deployment. We installed the sensors on one critical pump, knowing we were venturing into uncharted territory. Unexpected data patterns. Almost immediately, the sensor provided real-time data that revealed not only the anticipated early warning signs but also unexpected fluctuation and pump performance under varying loads.

These unforeseen data trends in system dynamics led us to discover that our existing maintenance protocols were missing subtle signs and stress during peak operations. We also found that the sensor placement and data transition setup needed adjustment for more accurate readings.

So, after all this, a valuable outcome has arrived. The process redesign, the pilot taught us, reached our approach to pump maintenance. We incorporated new data analytics, which allowed us to anticipate a failure before it escalated.

Then, in our system integration, we refined our sensor installation strategy and integrated a more robust data validation process, ensuring our monitoring system was both reliable and scalable.

The cultural shift, more importantly, the experience underscored the value of experimentation and agile decision making, reminding us that sometimes valuable insight comes from taking calculated risks even if we are not 100% ready. By embracing the start before you are ready, the mindset will solve an immediate problem and lay the groundwork for a proactive maintenance culture that includes overall operational efficiency.

At some point, we were deep into a project to upgrade a municipal water treatment plant with a new chemical dosing system designed to optimize desensitization while reducing operation costs. Midway through implementation, a series of unexpected regulatory challenges were announced that tightened chemical discharge limits.

There are multiple causes that have led to this, like:

1. The regulatory overall new discharge limits meant our planned system might not meet future standards, risking compliance and a costly retrofit.

2. Competitive innovation: The competitive digital solution not only improved efficiency but also integrated real-time data analytics, offering a proactive edge that resonated well with regulators and customers.

3. Rapid reassessment, i.e., we quickly gathered our technical regulatory teams to analyze the impact of those changes and evaluate alternative technology.

4. Revised strategy: we decided to pivot from a purely chemical-based approach to a hybrid solution that integrated advanced digital monitoring with a more sustainable treatment method. This meant handling the original plan mid-execution and redirected resources to develop a pilot project centered on

real-time data analytics, predictive maintenance and modified treatment protocol.

5. Throughout the pivot, we maintained close communication with both regulatory bodies and our customer base, explaining the rationale behind the change and how it could lead to better compliance and operational performance in the long term.

After all of this, there are multiple differences you may notice in the company's performance:

- **Enhance compliance and efficiency:** The updated method fulfilled the regulatory upgrade requirements and achieved a 35% decrease in energy and chemical consumption in the following year.

- **Market position:** We can rebrand ourselves as innovators in digital transformation in the water industry, which helps attract new business opportunities and partnerships.

- **Long-term resilience:** The experienced understand the importance of agility. By embracing a radical pivot when necessary, our organization can adapt quickly to shifting industry features.

Managing Cash Flow and Risks

If management and agility keep the company flowing, adopting sound financial habits is like the blood of the company, keeping it alive and pumping. It is incredibly vital to long-term business sustainability. I can share a few key practices that make a significant difference.

- Regress cash flow management, regular monitoring, and reuse our cash flow daily or weekly to identify trends and potential shortfalls early.

- Robust budgeting and forecasting, aka detailed budgets, develop comprehensive budgeting that covers all aspects of our operation, from capital expenditures to day-to-day expenses.

- Set aside a contingency reserve for unforeseen costs and market shifts.

- Regularly run different financial scenarios to test business models under varying conditions.

- Conduct regular audits of our expenses to identify potential areas for cost reduction without compromising quality.

- Invest in process, automation, and efficiency measures that can reduce costs and improve profitability long-term.

- Explore opportunities to diversify income sources and mitigate the risk of dependency on a single revenue stream.

- Consider offering new services or products that align with market demand, ensuring a buffer against market volatility.

This financial lab helps navigate day-to-day challenges and builds resilience, ensuring our business remains agile and prepared for future opportunities and uncertainties. This ensures a healthy balance sheet.

One key decision was to secure a flexible line of credit and restructure our operating expenses during unexpected regulatory and market challenges.

The sudden regulatory change led to a tight discharge standard of effluent, which disrupted our cash flow and increased operational costs. With revenue squeezed and pressure mounting on investment, in new compliance measures, we face the risk of a liquidity crunch.

One lesser-known practice is reverse stress testing. Instead of asking how much stress can be handled, we ask what extreme condition would cause our business to fail. This approach forces us to identify hidden vulnerable abilities in our financial model that might otherwise be overlooked.

Other specific practices include the Monte Carlo simulation. We run thousands of scenarios to forecast potential cash flow computation, which helps us understand 10 risks and plan contingency reserves.

We decided to risk map emerging factors. Instead of sticking solely to historical risks, we map emerging risks like sudden regulatory shifts to supply chain disruption using a dynamic risk matrix that gets updated regularly.

Scenario analysis with sensory testing involves alerting key variables such as interest rate, commodity prices, or regulatory fees. One at a time, we gain insight into which factors significantly impact our bottom line.

We also dig deeper into our insurance policies to uncover any hidden exposures or coverage gaps that might affect our financial stability during unforeseen events. This proactive approach provides a more complete picture of our risk landscape and enables us to make more informed decisions based on resilient financial strategies.

The First 90 Days – Creating an Action Plan

Over the next 90 days, our tracking mix for operational finance and strategic matrix can give me a well-rounded view of progress. Here, I want to specify some matrices that should be considered. I can explain.

In the operational matrix, monitor equipment uptime, downtime, and pump and treatment system reliability to see if initiatives like predictive maintenance reduce unexpected outages.

1. **Process efficiency:** Track flow rates, chemical usage, and energy consumption per water-treated unit. This can help evaluate the efficiency improvement resulting from a process fix or the implementation of new technology.

2. **Quality matrix:** Regularly take into account water quality parameters and discharge levels to ensure regulatory compliance and maintain or improve them.

3. **Financial matrix:** Cash flow and operating margins. Liquidity should be closely monitored, particularly when implementing a cost-saving initiative or new project.

4. **Cost saving:** Identify and quantify savings from operational improvement or renegotiated contracts.

5. **Return on investment, or ROI:** Measure the ROI for any pilot project or new technology to validate its potential and scalability.

The strategic and innovation matrix, pilot project milestone. If we are testing new technology like digital monitoring or AI-driven predictive maintenance, track key milestones such as installation, completion, data accuracy rates, early performance indicators, and customer borrowers' stakeholder feedback. We gather regulatory feedback from operators, regulatory bodies, and partners to assess the impact of changes and identify areas for future improvement. Employee engagement, major team training, and adoption rates of new tools or processes engaged teams can be a leading indicator of successful change implementation. By monitoring this matrix, we quickly identify what is working and what needs adjustment, and we ensure that our strategic initiative remains aligned with our long-term goals.

There was a time when our team embarked on a pilot project to implement digital modeling for a critical wastewater pump station. The goal was to test predictive maintenance using real-time data from IoT sensors, a new concept for our organization. The early win was what we wanted: a pilot implementation. We installed a sensor on a single high-impact pump that had a stream of unplanned downtime.

The immediate impact you witness is that the system detected early warning signs of abnormal vibration and temperature fluctuation within just a few weeks. Acting on this data, the maintenance team proactively addressed minor issues before escalating.

The pump performance improved noticeably, reducing downtime and avoiding what would have been a costly emergency repair.

This boosts team morale and momentum, builds confidence, sees the immediate benefits of implementing a relatively small investment, instills confidence in the technology and the team's ability to innovate, and creates positive energy.

Early wins galvanize the team's sparkly increased enthusiasm for exploring other digital solutions and process improvement.

This early win improved operational efficiency and reinforced the culture of proactive innovation and data-driven decision-making. It was a powerful reminder that taking calculated risks and acting on new ideas, even on a small scale, leads to significant moral-boosting success.

A concrete piece of advice is to break our 90-day plan into weekly sprints and establish daily accountability rituals. I can suggest a few steps for these:

i. Weekly Sprint: Take the process one week at a time, instead of letting yourself be overwhelmed by the pressing need to accomplish as much as possible. Pace yourself by taking it a week at a time, setting goals for one week, and trying different strategies for seven days. That is how you make the most of the 90 days.

ii. Daily accountability: Write down goals and tasks, and keep track of those goals and your own work. If you haven't been able to finish a task you thought you could have, examine why and try to find errors or mistakes in your approach. Constantly study your own habits and decisions.

iii. Track progress visually: Use a graph, log (digital or handwritten), or even a whiteboard to maintain a visual representation of your progress and future tasks. Using a visual element will help you reconfirm and plan without feeling overwhelmed by paragraphs of text.

By breaking the plan into manageable chunks and establishing daily review habits, you create a system of accountability and momentum that keeps you moving forward consistently.

The Role of Mentorship, Community, and Continuous Learning

If we have contacts in academic or research settings related to the environment, water, and wastewater engineering, academic researchers and mentors offer themselves as long-term prospects. Emerging technologies and trends can also be significant.

Finding the right mentor or accountable partner often starts by identifying someone experienced and aligned with your goals. Then, you reach out to a conventional mutual about mutual growth, someone in your network who is impressed with your insight or approach. Someone with a similar goal often makes a good mentor.

One effective strategy is to tap into your existing professional network. When discussing networks, seasonal industry colleagues, consider reaching out to senior engineers or managers at our current or past organization who have navigated similar challenges. Their hands-on experience in water and wastewater operations can provide practical insight.

Then, professional associations leverage connections from organizations like the American Water Association and Global Water Intelligence. Often, these groups have a membership program or network events where we can meet industry veterans who are willing to offer guidance.

Peer accountability partnerships, i.e., sometimes pairing with a peer, someone in a similar role from another organization, can be especially valuable during this process. Setting up a regular check-in to share progress, discuss challenges, and hold each other accountable allows you to be more focused and hold yourself more accountable.

At a local water webinar hosted by a regional water professional, we connected with a municipal utility head who is grappling with increasing water losses and aging distribution systems. During the initial interaction during the webinar and QA session, I shared some insight about how real-time sensor data would help detect leaks early.

After the session, we connected on LinkedIn and scheduled a meeting to explore the idea further. I presented a tailored proposal for a remote lead detection pilot program in an in-person meeting, including data projection and potential cost savings. Based on that discussion, a business approach was created.

Then, we launched a pilot project. Convinced by the proposal, the utility head initiated a small-scale pilot at a critical section of their network. Then, we tried to run the pilot successfully.

The pilot validated technology by reducing water loss by a significant margin and demonstrated improved operational efficiency.

Then, this partnership goes to a long-term partnership. Impressed by the pilot's success, the utility expanded the project to cover additional areas and ultimately introduced a multi-year contract for system-wide implementation.

This experience clearly illustrates how engaging with the community network led directly to a tangible business opportunity.

Network provides a platform to exchange ideas, gain trust, and ultimately turn a casual interaction into a successful, scalable business solution. That is the experience I can share.

Key Reader Takeaways

- A clear roadmap is the key to turning entrepreneurial ideas into reality.

- Execution matters more than perfection—taking action is the differentiator.

- Financial discipline and strategic planning are essential for long-term growth.

- A 90-day action plan helps create momentum and measurable progress.

- Mentorship, continuous learning, and community support accelerate success.

Commit to Your Roadmap

Reflection Exercise:

- Write down your long-term vision and break it into three key goals.

- Identify one action you will take toward your vision in the next 24 hours.

- Choose one area where you need mentorship or learning and seek guidance.

Commit to executing your 90-day action plan and track progress with weekly check-ins.

This is not the end—it's the beginning of your journey as an entrepreneur. You now have the tools, the strategies, and the mindset to navigate challenges, build strong teams, embrace innovation, and create a lasting impact.

The next step is up to you. Will you take it?

Conclusion

Your Journey – The Time to Act

Now that you've reached this point, your mind may be racing with ideas, possibilities, and plans for the future. You must have absorbed the lessons, the strategies, and the insights. You now stand at a crossroads—one path leads to action, momentum, and the realization of your entrepreneurial vision. The other leads to hesitation, uncertainty, and staying in the comfort zone. Which one will you choose?

The sticking point of my journey was the fact that I didn't just read about success—I relentlessly took deliberate action, overcame obstacles, built strong teams, and led with purpose. Now, it's your turn. The knowledge from this book means nothing unless it is applied.

This book has provided the blueprint for entrepreneurial success, but only you can bring it to life. The most important factor in achieving your goals is the decision to act now.

Revisiting the Core Lessons of This Book

Before we part ways, let's discuss all the points we've touched on, for a little memory jog and reinforcement.

In **Chapter 1**, we covered the choice of making that first step and considered the idea of stepping into a completely new realm.

In **Chapter 2**, we discussed crafting the approach and the main goal that would act as a compass in your journey.

Chapter 3 was about teams and people, and how they act like a stable platform that can only help make the journey less rocky.

Chapter 4 encountered the topic of leadership and how one can become the captain of one's ship.

Chapter 5 dealt with the art of dealing with challenges, and how to make sure it didn't knock you off balance.

And for **Chapter 6**, we discussed how connections and fellow startup leaders can help you out through this journey.

Chapter 7 efficiently tackled innovation and how necessary the skill of pivoting and creativity is for startups.

Chapter 8 was all about legacy and how to leave your mark in history.

Finally, **Chapter 9** wrapped it all up with a step-by-step rehash of a roadmap to success.

Apart from this, you will have learnt:

- Entrepreneurship is about embracing uncertainty and taking bold steps.

- Leadership is not just about running a business—it's about inspiring and guiding others.

- Success is built on relationships, adaptability, and continuous learning.

The Importance of Taking Immediate Action
1. Perfection = Inaction

An "all-or-nothing" ideology only sabotages your chance to ever make your dreams come true. You may be the most disciplined and motivated person, but the more you tell yourself you'll wait, the more you set your timeline back. The "perfect time" is a myth and simply doesn't exist.

If there is any bit of a perfect time that exists, it's now. So all you need to take away from this is one thing: *Carpe Diem, Seize the Day!*

2. Consistency is Key

Consistency is a severely underrated skill, one that people overlook all the time. No matter how much talent or skill one holds in life, if they cannot be consistent and keep at it at a regular pace

The Journey is Ongoing — Commit to Lifelong Learning

The best entrepreneurs out there never stop growing, evolving, and learning. Sometimes people might think that entrepreneurship is up to natural talent or genius, when that couldn't be further from the truth. Anyone can have ideas, but execution takes skill, grit, and most of all, consistency. You can have all the talent in the world, but consistency is a skill that needs to be honed regularly and put to work every day. It's not cheap and takes what it needs. But that's exactly what gets you to those big stages.

By actively working on your communication, confidence, collaboration, curiosity, and comfort with the unknown, you can steadily build yourself into a leader who knows exactly what they want and how to climb up to achieve that.

The last thing I can leave you with now is a few questions that will further help you introspect on your process and goals for your journey. Like:

- What is your first action step after finishing this book?

- What are the biggest lessons you've learned from this journey?

- How will you measure your progress in the next six months?

- What fears or doubts still hold you back, and how will you overcome them?

At the end of the day, the biggest difference between successful entrepreneurs and others is action.

Key Readers Takeaways:
- Leadership, financial discipline, and innovation must be continuously practiced.

- Mentorship, relationships, and impact are as important as profitability.

- Your entrepreneurial journey is ongoing—commit to learning and evolving.

Take the First Step Today:
- Commit to your first business goal today.

- Share your vision with a mentor, advisor, or business partner.

- Start implementing your 90-day action plan now.

The only thing standing between you and success is action. You have the knowledge, the tools, and the strategies—now go and *build something extraordinary.*

About the Author

Dr. Surendra Sambhaji Takawale is a distinguished Indian entrepreneur and chemical engineer, renowned for his transformative contributions to sustainable water and wastewater management. With nearly three decades of experience, he has consistently demonstrated strategic leadership and innovation in the environmental sector.

Educational and Professional Background

Dr. Takawale's academic journey is marked by excellence and a commitment to continuous learning. He holds a degree in chemical engineering, which laid the foundation for his technical expertise. Further enhancing his strategic acumen, he pursued advanced management studies at the Indian Institute of Management (IIM) Ahmedabad and the Saïd Business School, University of Oxford. Additionally, he earned a Ph.D. in Strategy & Business Management, underscoring his dedication to academic rigor and strategic thinking.

Leadership at Blue Zone Ventures

As the Executive Director and Co-founder of Blue Zone Ventures Private Limited, Dr. Takawale has been instrumental in pioneering innovative solutions in water and wastewater management. Under his leadership, the company specializes in:

- **Utility Management:** Comprehensive operation and maintenance of water and wastewater treatment facilities.

- **Asset Management:** Upgrading existing facilities and implementing advanced automation projects.

- **Industrial Water Solutions (IWS):** Customized solutions for industrial challenges, including specialty chemicals and the implementation of the Transfer-Operate-Transfer (T-O-T) model for efficient water management.

Dr. Takawale emphasizes the integration of automation and AI to enhance sustainability and customer satisfaction, positioning Blue Zone Ventures at the forefront of technological advancement in the industry.

Recognitions and Achievements

Dr. Takawale's visionary leadership has been recognized through numerous accolades, including:

- National Achievers Award for Business Excellence (2021)

- Highflyers 50 Award (2022)

- Business Leader of the Year Award

- CEO of the Year – Indian Achievers Award

- 10 Best CEOs in India 2023 by Trade Flock magazine

- Business Leadership 2023 by Brand Global Med

- Rashtriya Udyog Ratna Award